Reflections

Cal Bombay

REFLECTIONS

CAL BOMBAY

Reflections

Printed in Canada
International Standard Book Number: 978-1-894860-53-6
ISBN 978-1-927355-05-3 EPUB, ISBN 978-1-927355-06-0 PDF

Published by:
Castle Quay Books
1307 Wharf Street, Pickering, Ontario, L1W 1A5
Tel: (416) 573-3249
E-mail: info@castlequaybooks.com www.castlequaybooks.com

Copy edited by Marina H. Hofman Willard
Cover design by Burst Impressions
Interior layout and design by Diane Roblin-Lee
Printed at Essence Printing, Belleville, Ontario

Library and Archives Canada Cataloguing in Publication

Bombay, Cal, 1937-
Reflections / Cal Bombay.
Issued also in electronic formats.
ISBN 978-1-894860-53-6
1. Christian life. 2. Bombay, Cal, 1937-. I. Title.
BV4501.3.B64 2012 248.4 C2012-901726-4

Castle Quay Books

Table of Contents

Foreword

If there is one thing that people appreciate and value in public communications these days it is authenticity. There are so many voices in our multifaceted world of books, TV shows, Facebook, Twitter, e-mails, and texting that it is almost impossible to discern what is and isn't of value. We're awash in opinion and theory but lacking in proven experience and trustworthy track-record. This is why I'm so impressed with Cal Bombay's newest book, *Reflections*. Cal writes from a position of strength in terms of character, personal history and integrity. For over 50 years, he has faithfully "ground it out" in the Lord's work in Africa and Canada. Today, after 25 years of national television prominence, he has become a champion to the infant nation of South Sudan, and is so trusted that he has spoken to the south Sudanese parliament, where a standing ovation culminated in a motion to give him citizenship. I've known Cal for decades. He is a man of integrity who has walked where few of us will ever go. He writes beautifully. He paints compelling word pictures and draws the reader into his vast world of adventure. You're going to love this book.

James Cantelon

100 Huntley Street Co-host
President of *Visionledd*

Introduction

Reflecting on the past can be thrilling, humbling, shocking and instructive.

God turns up in the most amazing places. When the shock and shaking are finished after a frightening experience, one can recognize that God was there. When a thundering thought seems to come out of the blue, one can recognize that God popped something into the mind. I can almost imagine God waiting and watching for our reaction. At the same time, we can be fully assured of His guidance and presence in tough circumstances.

Life can come to the place where a calmness and peace prevails. We can be certain that, though new challenges are faced, that peace and confidence will remain.

The reflections I relate in this book are sometimes incidental, yet significant. Others are thoughts which abruptly took full form. Well into my seventies now, I still shudder at what might have been had God not been present.

I look back and wonder. What I write in these following pages is very deliberate. The situations and experiences might seem unlikely, but every word is true in fact, in location and time.

Life has always been right in my face and challenging. Fear has never been a part of it. Forward is the only direction I know to go, and I like it that way.

I always contemplate the next surprise event, knowing that God will handle the hard stuff, while I remain obedient in the small stuff. Life with God goes on and on.

Meanwhile I'll pick up some of the files which fell out of my memory and relate them in a way that illustrates that God is always there, sometimes unrealized.

These are not my memoirs. I'll write those in my eighties. So many memories yet to be constructed in life!

Cal Bombay

1 Contentment

A rifle was pressed against my right temple. I had stopped driving because a large tree was lying across the dirt road in Uganda. Men in soldiers' uniforms had jumped out of the gutters beside the road and surrounded me. They turned out to be Idi Amin's troops and they were probably set to rob me. I had no idea what to do. They kept yelling at me with threatening gestures in a language I did not understand. It went on for some time. I pretended to be calm.

I tried to talk to them in English, Kiswahili and the little Luganda I spoke, but they seemed to understand none of it. Finally, I pointed at my chest, then at a mission visible on a hill in the distance and repeatedly said, "Padre." It worked!

They seemed to understand that I had some association with the mission, and they backed off, dragging the tree out of my way. I drove off with some trembling and a great deal of wonder and relief. I knew Idi Amin's troops were getting little financial support and were stealing food from innocent Ugandan small farmers. There was great discontent and fear throughout the whole country. Already thousands had died. I was a survivor.

John the Baptist gave his instructions to soldiers once. In Luke 3:14 we read where they asked him, *"And what shall we do?"* So he said to them, *"Do not intimidate anyone or accuse falsely, and be content with your wages."*

If that Scripture had come to mind and **if** they had been able to understand me and **if** I had courage and calmness of mind I **might** have quoted that to them – a lot of ifs!

Where do you suppose discontent has its genesis? Not just in soldiers, but in most of us! I think if we read James 4:1-6 it will become quite clear. We in our western society don't seem like a very content lot of people. Paul wrote in 1 Timothy 6:6, *"godliness with contentment is great gain."* Philippians 4:11-12, as well as Hebrews 13:5, instruct us as Christians to not be covetous, but to be content with what we have.

I've seen great poverty in many parts of the world. Most of those people have similar needs: food, shelter, clothes, education. Yet even some of them seem content with their lot. Paul says in 1 Timothy 6:8, *"And having food and clothing, with these we shall be content."*

Strange, but I've rarely seen that in North America! Is it wrong to be rich? No! On the other hand, is it right to be self-centred and indulgent to the degree we are here in North America?

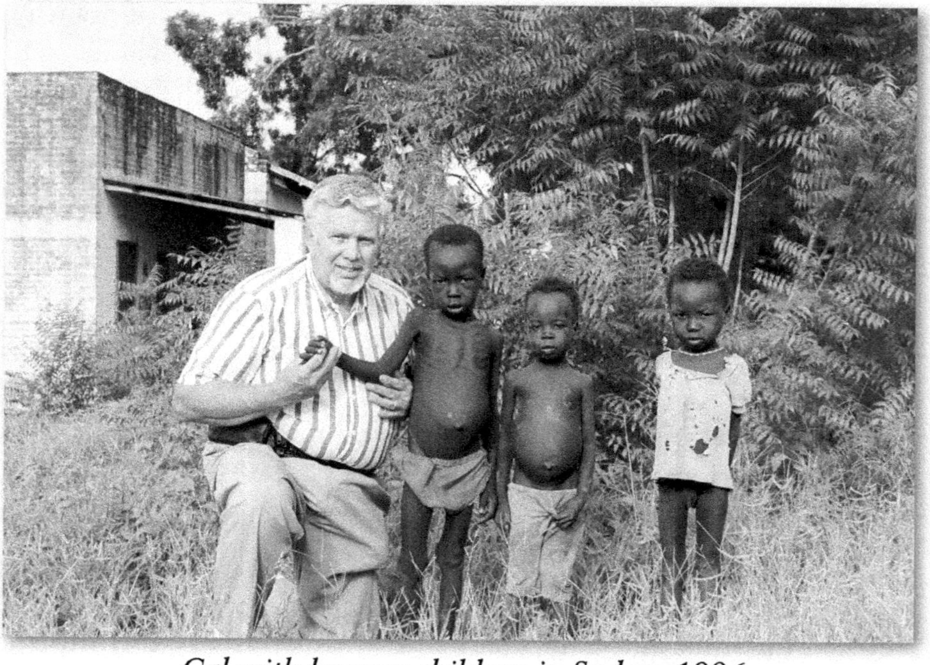

Cal with hungry children in Sudan, 1996

2 Deference

I was in Nigeria at the time.

Flying in and out of Nigeria is hectic at the best of times. When I had arrived, the congestion both at the airport and on the roads to the centre of Lagos was beyond imagination. My friend Samuel Odunaike, an executive with Shell Oil, had come to pick me up. Samuel had agreed to write a book for me to publish in Kenya. Now it had taken eight hours to reach his office in downtown Lagos.

It was hot. Really hot! I was there for only a few days in ministry, then had to go on to Ghana. And that's when it happened.

When my flight was announced I got up to walk across the tarmac to the stairs up into the aircraft. Everyone had assigned seats, but there was such a rush and crush that I was at the back of another congestion—a seething mass of people pushing and pulling at one another to get up those stairs first and into a seat. I had never seen such a scrum, not even on a rugby field. As I walked up and into the plane, last, I found that my seat was filled to overflowing with a large lady with a defiant look on her face and her great arms wrapped around a pile of possessions, some spilling onto me as I sat down.

> Take the low seat, and let God work you up from there. Fighting for your own rights isn't near as comfortable and long-lasting as being "put in place" by God.

I turned to a flight attendant with no words but a question in my eyes. I was quite ready to defer to the overflow beside me, since it was just a two hour flight, but the attendant smiled at me, returned later and led me into first class and gave me a better seat than I had paid for. First class had been closed when the scrum began, and there were a few empty seats. I got first class treatment for the whole trip.

Deference! Sounds like an old-fashioned word, doesn't it? Giving place to someone else when it could have—perhaps *should* have been—your own right. Not always an easy thing to do. But, as Christians we are sometimes *forced* to act like Christians.

Both Romans 12:10 and Philippians 2:3 seem pertinent to this situation. But I was, in a sense, forced to defer to someone else in this situation. Then I thought of what Jesus said in Luke 14:10-11. Take the low seat, and let God work you up from there. Fighting for your own rights isn't near as comfortable and long-lasting as being "put in place" by God.

Deference is for the short term. The reward is for the full journey, first class!

3
Forgiveness

I was ambushed a few years ago in South Sudan, along with the party travelling with me. AK-47s threatened us. We were robbed, but we got away with our lives plus a few other things I demanded back while the two guns were pointed directly at me. But that is another story.

In the days following, we kept in touch with the authorities. After a few days we heard that two of the four bandits had been apprehended and were being held in custody at the border back near Uganda, where we were to return a few days later. They had also recovered all but the money which we had lost in the incident.

> "Judge not, and you shall not be judged. Condemn not, and you shall not be condemned."
> Luke 6:37

I asked Dr. Samson Kwaje, Minister of Information, and one of the victims of the ambush if I could have a word with these thieves when we reached the Sudan side of the border where they were being held. He wondered why I wanted to talk with them. I told him simply that I wanted to tell them that I forgave them. He made arrangements by radio. When we arrived near the Uganda border we were escorted to the grass-roofed, windowless mud hut where they were locked in and confined by leg shackles.

The police brought them to us under a massive mango tree, and a crowd began to gather around us. I told them quite clearly that I forgave them. I also told them why. I referred to the biblical requirement I have as a Christian, mentioned in Luke 6:37. *"Judge not, and you shall not be judged. Condemn not, and you shall not be condemned. Forgive, and you will be forgiven."* I also told them that God would also forgive them of *all* their sins if they would accept what Jesus did for them at Calvary.

Forgiveness is not always easy. But with the Christian it is necessary. Some would like to hold on to the grudge, get even or use their bad experience as a reason to collect sympathy to support their bitterness.

Forgiveness was not easy for God! He sacrificed His own Son to provide a means for His grace to offer us forgiveness. That cost God a lot! But it bought Him a whole worldwide family of sons and daughters.

As one of those sons or daughters you can do yourself a great deal more good by forgiving than by withholding forgiveness. It's the Christian thing to do.

4 Alone

Don flew me by helicopter onto the top of a mountain in the Canadian Rockies. He landed, let me out and left me on the flat, snow-covered top of one of the highest mountains around. I was wearing a Hudson's Bay coat with its red, yellow and green stripes around it. Don flew away and down, out of sight and hearing. We had planned that he would fly past me with my cameraman hanging out the door to take video as he flew past.

He didn't come back. After about twenty minutes, I started to feel abandoned, forsaken, alone! It was perfectly still, and windless. The quiet of the mountains has a certain eerie sound. It's something like a hum mixed with a whisper. It inspired awe. After more time had passed, it took on a sense of quiet foreboding. It was cold. I became somewhat anxious. I felt totally alone. Had Don forgotten me or which mountain I was on? Had he crashed? He had a competent reputation. I was starting to freeze.

Without the slightest warning a roar filled my ears as the helicopter rose above the edge of the flat of the mountaintop. I had heard nothing coming until it was right there in my face.

Suddenly and often when the last hope is slipping away, God arrives with thunderous presence...

I know a few people who have gone through a similar experience, but with God. They felt like God had forsaken them. I have been in that same state of mind and spirit: not quite certain that God is still out there—somewhere—maybe.

Yet, Jesus made a promise that He would never leave us or forsake us.

Sometimes it doesn't feel that way, since circumstances and experience seems to smother the fact, drawing a veil over our trust. Jesus felt something like that on the cross. "Why have you forsaken Me?"

Time always proves the promise of Jesus to be true. Suddenly and often when the last hope is slipping away, God arrives with thunderous presence, and all loneliness is swept away as He gently settles down beside you and takes you into His arms.

And it's so warm.

5 God Is Punishing Me

I'm sure this doesn't come as a surprise to anyone, but I have done some rather wrong things in my life. Some of them could probably be categorized as sin. OK, I'll be totally honest—they were sin. I don't need to name them. Some may not have been sin in the biblical sense, but they were certainly wrong according to my understanding of the Bible and how we should live, talk and act.

For one example, I skipped paying my tithes for a period of time, considering my own needs too pressing to be able to afford to tithe. I have since discovered that I cannot afford not to tithe. Some people consider this a controversial issue. I don't. For I have found that when I tithe, God blesses me.

But I got it into my head that God was punishing me when I had stopped tithing for that period. Everything seemed to go wrong, including some financial matters. I rather think now that God simply withheld the blessings He promised to pour out on those who bring the tithe to God's provision house, the church.

In any case it somehow seemed connected to my tithing or not tithing, at least in my mind. I was convinced that God loved me but in this case was also chastising me. And the Bible does say that God does that.

In my final analysis of this situation, and in many others, I have come to the assessment that I am personally responsible for my own hard times. I suppose indirectly God is responsible since He fashioned the order of the universe, but I was responsible myself for disregarding those principles. I knew better, but disregarded the better, and brought the consequences down on my own head.

I can't blame God for my wrongdoing. Nor can I even blame the devil. He gets too much credit already.

I am a responsible individual, and I must live responsibly and obediently.

6 Will We Die?

Someday I will die. That and taxes are inevitable. The questions that often plague most of us are when, how and will it be painful?

In Kenya I thought that moment had come for Mary and me. In fact it was a matter of choice. It was not suicidal, but rational. It was sudden and qualified as an emergency.

Two buses side by side, billowing clouds of black diesel exhaust, loaded beyond reason, overcrowded with people, were in a race. They were chugging uphill approaching the brow of the hill just as I was driving up the other side. Driving on the left side of the road is legal. Driving on both sides in a race was not. There were no posted speed limits. The road conditions limited speed all by themselves. The buses were not going more than 60 km per hour. I was doing perhaps 90 km.

As the situation crystallized in my mind I knew I had to make a choice—and fast! Pull off the road to the left or hit one of the

Family photo in Kenya

buses head-on. It was a difficult choice. To my left was a sheer cliff dropping hundreds of feet, and the verge was just a few feet wide. To the right, a sheer rock cut and a narrow verge. Was it Mary and I and two busloads who would die or just Mary and I? I instinctively pulled off to the left, at speed.

My left tires bobbled and bounced on a row of whitewashed stones at the very edge, then were silent. I had gone too far. In a flash the buses were past, and I turned the wheels to get back on the road. The tires bounced again on the row of whitewashed stones, and we bounced back onto the road. We stopped farther down the hill beside the road, both of us trembling.

Later, when we looked at the row of stones we realized that there was nothing but a sheer drop beyond them. They were right on the edge. There simply was not enough room for a full-width car to pass without going over the edge. Our tires had been riding on air. Do you suppose Deuteronomy 33:27 has anything to do with this?

And people wonder why I believe in angels!

7 Friendliness

I was approached by a total stranger who, with no introduction, came out with the statement, "I want to be your friend." I was slightly taken back, wondering on what basis this friendship could be built. And, what was the motive? Let's face it. Rarely does a friendship start without the process of time. I would like to know someone before I consider them a real friend.

We all have friends. Some remain from our youth and some are from our adult life. A few are very close friends; others are not. Some are near; some are distant. Some are black and some are white.

I have two closest friends, one black and one white. And I have hundreds of others of many races whom I hold as friends. But all these friendships developed over time.

Friendship doesn't just happen. Yet, friendships are essential and must be developed over time for trust and relationships to grow in a proper and lasting way (Proverbs 18:24). Those are the "close" friendships which last for life.

I've met people whom I'd not set out to make friends. Their attitude, demeanour and voice would instantly freeze-dry the possibility. Proverbs 22:24-25 says: "*Make no friendship with an angry man, And with a furious man do not go, Lest you learn his ways And set a snare for your soul.*"

Friendships should be for the sake of friendship alone, without ulterior motives (Proverbs 14:20) and with very great care (Proverbs 12:26).

The great contradiction to all this is literally an act of God. He sent His Son Jesus Christ to be a friend of sinners (like you and me) and even those whom society demeans and despises (such as tax collectors).

So where does that leave me as a Christian?

To take a risk and, through developing friendships, earn the right to talk candidly and openly about the Friend who sticks closer than a brother. Christians can be friends of the worldly without having to be friends of the world.

8 Origins

Mary and I were married in January 1959. You can imagine the shock I got when I discovered, 21 years after our anniversary, in 1980, that I had married my cousin.

You see, a scientist was quoted in an article years ago by Jack Miller in the *Toronto Star*. Part of that article said this:

"WE REALLY ARE ONE BIG FAMILY

"We are related, you and I, whoever you are. You may not be my sister or brother, but you are at least my cousin—however far removed. You can be from any race, from any place—it's no matter. We're family. That's the latest scientific theory, and it's backed by the surprising results of impressive research. It says evidence in our genes shows there really was an EVE—a universal grandmother—even if we have no scientific sign yet of Adam."

Cal with Mary's family

So obviously I married my very distant cousin, no matter how far removed. And let's face it, so did you and every married person you know!

The results of this research seem to have been a surprise to genetic researchers. They have samples of tissue from 147 women from all around the world, and by tracing the mitochondria were able to prove conclusively that Eve (yes, the scientists chose that name) was the common single ancestor to the whole human race. She did in fact exist.

That article also makes the following statement: *"this was a real person, not just some theoretical ancestor. So all eight or nine billion humans on Earth today are her descendants."*

So, what does that have to do with anything? Precisely this! The more advanced science becomes, the more it falls into line with the statements of Scripture. While the number of scientists who believe in creation is growing, the number of scientists who promote evolution are diminishing, or at least have now become doubtful of the theory of evolution.

The more advanced science becomes, the more it falls into line with the statements of Scripture. ... The number of scientists who promote evolution are diminishing...

How improbable that the writers of the various books of the Bible could have come to their conclusions through scientific research! The marvels of modern scientific research were not available to them. What else can we conclude but that their writings were by revelation from God? Notice what is written in 2 Timothy 3:16: *"All Scripture is given by inspiration of God."*

That settles your physical ancestry.

9 Faith

I may have seen it all when it comes to "faith." What an abused term!

I preached under a big mango tree near a town called Soroti, in Uganda, where I saw 17 clear miracles of God's healing and deliverance, from blind eyes opened to a teenager delivered from demonic possession and control. In the same meeting, about three hundred people received Jesus as Lord and Saviour. This was all a result of the biblical, child-like faith we should have as believers.

I have also seen people demand that God should heal them because they were given some sort of formula which God was bound to honour. And yet no healing came! I have also seen people who were not healed who one would have thought deserved it. This is the result of faith in "faith," rather than childlike faith in God. I have also seen those whom one would think did not deserve healing yet were healed.

The Bible records that once when Jesus healed people great rejoicing took place, while others were scandalized because it was not done on the proper day.

As adults, most of us, unlike children, feel it is somewhat bold to ask for a gift. How many of us would ask someone whom we rarely even talk with to give us a new car? How many of us spend time in God's Word and in prayerful conversation with God? It does say clearly in Romans 10:17 that there is a relationship between faith and our minding the Word of God. Faith is a gift of God.

Though many books have been written about faith, it still seems to me that taking the Bible at its face value is by far a better bulwark than the many private interpretations of Scripture we see these days.

It may be that our greatest problem when it comes to faith is that we have become self-centred about it, rather than God-centred. Have we have forgotten that He is Sovereign?

"I want from God what I want from God." To adapt what President John Kennedy once said, "Ask not what God can do for you, but what you should do for God!"

Perhaps it's about time we considered what God wants from us. And THAT is when faith has its greatest challenge. You see, God has a bigger plan than we can even comprehend. You and I are not the centre of that plan—God is!

10 Dancing on Snakes

In Kenya, a few beautiful miles up the hills above Lake Victoria, is a mission established in 1911 by Otto Keller. His grave is located there in a beautifully flowered garden. A path leads through that garden from the Bible college at which I was teaching, to the mud-filled walls of the house where Mary and I were living.

I'd seen most breeds of snakes after I'd been in Kenya for a few years, and generally they will slither way from you with more fear than you. I repeat, "generally" they'll make their escape. I say this because one day while walking that garden path I inadvertently stepped right on top of two green mambas. I looked down to see what squishy feeling was under my shoe. I saw their heads and bodies thrashing about. I have trod water when swimming but that was my first attempt at treading air. I was out of there in no time. Green mambas are deadly.

Home in Nairobi, Kenya

It never occurred to me at that excited moment, but I later realized that Psalm 91:13 applied to me when God's angels are around. *"You shall tread upon the lion and the cobra, the young lion and the serpent you shall trample underfoot."* It happened, but my heartbeat did speed up considerably as well.

Some might say I was just lucky. If that's the case, I've been "lucky" many more times than my share. Not just with snakes but with guns pointed at me, with narrow misses on narrow roads in Africa and with probably dozens of incidents of which I was unaware.

> God can and does send angels to protect us... and covers us with His wings.

That is simply because Psalm 91:11 is true. God can and does send angels to protect us, sets hedges about us and covers us with His wings. I don't think snakes know how to think, but if they could, they probably would have felt they were lucky to get away with their lives.

You can put the serpent on the run, you know! It depends on who you walk with.

11 Equity

I was standing in the middle of a refugee camp in Ethiopia. As I watched closely, a very thin man stooped into a little covering made from what might have been a bedsheet. He crawled in and a few moments later came out with his daughter in his arms, wrapped in a dirty white cloth. A stricken yet stoic look was on the man's face as he carried his little child to the common burial pit. I neither had the heart to have my cameraman point the camera in his direction nor followed him in his last short solemn trip with his little girl. She had succumbed in agony to starvation.

I stood there wondering on the problem of equity. Why was I, with my children, born in rich Canada, and this man and his daughter born into such a hopelessly war-torn and wretched situation in this part of the world? I was told all my life that all men were equal. Certainly that equality I was told about had to be at another level! Before God we are all equal. Yet, no matter the cause, death does level the playing field.

In Psalm 98:9, we read of God: *"For He is coming to judge the earth. With righteousness He shall judge the world, And the peoples with equity."*

Meanwhile, before He comes and because of the hearts of humankind, we live in a world of great inequity. That's just the way it is! But does that mean that as a Christian I should do nothing about it?

The apostle Paul wrote to Christians in Corinth that when we see others in need and we have abundance, we are called upon to "share the wealth." He was collecting from the Corinthian Christians from their abundance to supply the great lack among the Christians in Jerusalem. You can read about it in 2 Corinthians 8:12-15.

But reading about it does not produce equity. Doing something about it—sharing our wealth—does!

And this pleases God. You can read Proverbs 22:9 and get the message. Or, start reading at Matthew 25:34—then pause when you get to verse 45.

Equity starts in the heart: a heart obedient to God. If equity does not start with Christians, do you imagine a godless society will be able to force it by law?

12 Problems? No Problem!

There are some really daft people in the Church. You could call them flakes, fakes or heretics.

They teach, over radio, television (or in pulpits), a simple lie and purportedly back it all up with the Bible. What they teach is that if you do things right, live a perfect life before God and follow a certain series of steps of faith, then your troubles will be a thing of the past. The use such Scriptures as *"My God shall supply all your need according to His riches in glory by Christ Jesus"* (Philippians 4:19).

The Scriptures are true. I believe the Bible! What these heretics forget to mention is that God will supply all our *needs*, not all our desires and wishes. Someone may say, "I *wish* I had a million dollars," then say with added holy piety, "I'd even give most of it to the church!!" Right!

Do they forget that everyone, Christians and non-Christians alike, get head colds, aches and pains? (Though some might not admit it to protect their heresy!)

I could quote a dozen Scriptures which these people misuse to convince others they can have a blessed and easy life—and then they take up an offering. *"For the time will come when they will not endure sound doctrine; but after their own lusts shall they heap to themselves teachers, having itching ears"* (2 Timothy 4:3 KJV).

All this foolishness grates on my theological nerves! What about the fact that the Bible says *"Your Father...sends rain on the just and on the unjust"* (Matthew 5:45)? Or 2 Timothy 3:12 *"Yea, and all that will live godly in Christ Jesus shall suffer persecution"?*

Formulae do not work! But God's Word is powerful, and God can answer any prayer asked within His will. Forcing God into a corner with twisted theology is asking for trouble.

Better to ask God clearly what you want to ask and trust Him for that prayer to be answered.

If you want to have a problem-free life, you'll have to wait for the return of Christ in all His power and glory—at which time all tears (and heresies) will be wiped away. No problem!

13 Wealth and Wisdom

I was asked one time what I would do if I had a million dollars. My first reaction was "Fat chance!" Then I thought about it and said, "I'd spend some of it, give quite a bit away to worthy causes, lay some up for my old age and then go buy an ice cream cone."

One of the richest men in America was asked the question "How much money is enough?" His answer was: "Just a little bit more." That answer made me ponder just what might be revealed in his character and personality with such an answer. Ambition! Drive! Goals! Workaholism! Self-centeredness! Greed! What?

There is nothing wrong with being rich or even reaching the stage of being a multi-billionaire—as long as that wealth was gained in a lawful, ethical and honest way without abusing either people or society as a whole.

Being rich does not necessarily prove a person to be wise. Perhaps clever, knowledgeable, brilliant even, but not necessarily wise. Being rich and being wise is possible and commendable.

Our problem in thinking of wealthy people is the mistaken notion that they should be more highly respected and treated simply because of their riches. Indeed, wealthy people are often treated differently. It's unfortunate since it gives the wealthy person an inflated view of himself. To be rich and humble is difficult. I do know a few people who are both.

Here's the rub! Anyone who is preoccupied with stashing away "things" and lusts after money, gain and possessions is in fact robbing himself of all the simple joys of life, and lives in a self-produced vacuum. Proverbs 1:17-19 speak of this, and the last few words in these verses are: *"So are the ways of everyone who is greedy for gain; It takes away the life of its owners."*

Jesus reflected the same sentiment when He said that life is not made up of the abundance of *things* a person owns.

One thing I've observed: The wealthiest people I know are not the most happy. I've met people in real poverty who are truly happy. Ever wonder why?

Cal's family - October 2005

14 Be Still

Jack Lynn was one of the most effective and respected missionaries I ever knew. He spoke several Kenyan languages and was highly regarded by African leaders. He was older than me, and I looked on him as an example to emulate. Where I would lose patience, he seemed always to be able to hold his cool. If I had an idea and wanted another opinion, his would be the first I would seek. He loved Africa and Africans. We went hunting in Kenya's Rift Valley together a few times to get meat for our larders. He was fun, funny, fulfilled and full of serious wisdom. He was a straight shooter, both with a rifle and with his advice.

He could stand between two totally opposing views and eventually bring people together, whether individuals or tribal groups. He knew better than most when to be silent and when to speak. He also knew when to be still. Jack had a quiet confidence about him.

One night at his home in Embu, Kenya, he awakened in the night with a strange feeling. He felt coldness down the indentation along his backbone! A sheet was over him, mattress under him, and his wife beside him. He realized what it was and stayed absolutely still. Finally, with a slithering motion, the snake, which had obviously come for the warmth on Jack's back, slid out of his bed and away. I'm not sure what I'd have done under the circumstances or, as in this case, under the snake.

There are moments in all of our lives when we sense the presence of evil or danger or simply feel a strange anxiety. The mind begins to race and we try to figure out a way of escape or what to do to rid ourselves of this ominous and unknown threat.

It is at moments like that when we need to concentrate on one simple truth. In Matthew 28:20, Jesus says, *"to observe all things that I have commanded you; and lo, I am with you always, even to the end of the age."* Amen.

We need to note not only the promise of His presence, but the requirement to observe all that He taught and commanded. That's when we can relax even in dangerous circumstances, knowing not only that He is there but that He also knows what is best for us.

"Be still, and know that I am God" (Psalm 46:10).

15 Abrasions

In my little workshop, I have a machine called a grinding wheel. It has two sides to it. One side is a wire-wheel which can be used to clean rusty things and actually make them shine. The other, more oft used side has a three-quarter inch wide abrasive stone. It is rough and coarse and cuts into metal, throwing sparks in a stream down toward the floor. Both sides are abrasive enough to cause lots of scratches.

I don't store flammable liquids nearby. That could end in a heated argument with death.

Sometimes people leave scratches, mostly invisible. We've all met abrasive people. They can set off sparks without even thinking about it. Like the grinding wheel, the whole world spins around with themselves at the centre of their own attention, and the effect can be very intrusive. People don't like to be around them very much. The greater the pressure on them, the more sparks fly. Often an explosion follows, words are exchanged and a quarrel begins. Yet perhaps we need a few of them around us to keep us clean and keen and to wear off some of our own sharp corners!

Some of these abrasive characters feel their whole calling in life is to criticise and correct everyone within sight and sound of them. Often what they say is right but the tone and attitude which they use drives people away, most often nullifying any "rightness" they may have expressed. They rarely do people any good, except to perhaps be a catalyst to the development of some patience.

The way people act dictates pretty much how others react. The apostle Paul knew this when he wrote to the young preacher in 2 Timothy 2:24-25, telling him to be gentle and to act in humility in correcting people. He went on to say that in this way, perhaps those doing wrong would repent and know the truth about themselves.

There would be many less explosions in our society if we were all to take that simple, biblical advice. Of course we need to be sure that we are not flammable material, looking for a fight, an explosion looking for a place to blow up.

On the other hand, I've had a few abrasions which were entirely my own doing. Sometimes we are our own hardest person to live with. A gentle spirit and humility are the remedy for both wrongs committed against us and those we often inflict on ourselves through thoughtless choice of words or actions.

16

His Word Is His Bond

Ever hear of the "good old days"? In spite of some modern denials of the value of "the good old days," there actually were some pretty good practices back then. The saying was still true: "A man's word is his bond." People borrowed thousands of dollars and committed to paying it back with a simple handshake. And they did pay it back. Courts deal with much of that stuff these days, even with signed documents.

In recent years it's become hard to trust people. Occasionally it's hard to trust yourself. A commitment made in a highly emotional circumstance can become a doubtful obligation down the road in a few days, weeks or years. It's not really that hard to rationalize our way out of an "insignificant" promise.

While listening to a preacher preach about sin, righteousness and judgment, people make commitments to a higher ethical and moral standard, often in a quiet unspoken way. When the preacher's gone and the conscience gets a little seared, a little memory slippage, a little tumble or a little excuse, and slowly a lesser standard seems acceptable.

It happens to many Christians, especially if they don't keep their minds on the Word of God. Without daily spiritual food together with meditation on the Word, standards have a tendency to be undernourished.

There are examples in the Bible of saying one thing and doing another. King Saul, for instance! When Samuel the prophet had died, Saul had already banished spiritualists and mediums from the land. But when he got into a tight spot, he disguised himself and went to a medium at Endor (1 Samuel 28:3-10). The experience was a bad one for Saul.

Cal Bombay

The apostle Paul had some pretty strong things to say on the matter in Romans 2:21-24. If you publicly decry stealing and adultery and yet your secret life is quite the opposite, you will eventually bring shame on yourself and the name of Jesus. The only cure for that is to repent and turn from your wickedness to receive God's forgiveness.

You see, God keeps His Word! What is there not to love about God?

17 Missing a Chance

I remember walking back into a gas station to return money to the cashier when I was given too much change. The surprised remark from the clerk was, "Man, I haven't seen that happen before!" It's not a boast. I was just brought up right. But this does illustrate our diminished expectation of higher values in our society.

In January 2005, I was officially invited to Kenya for the massive celebration of the Comprehensive Peace Agreement between the Islamist northern government of Sudan and the beleaguered and terrorized predominantly Christian south. It was a great celebration. The Bible was quoted often and freely in speeches by those of the south.

It became apparent that there were three major threats to the success of the south now that peace, at least on paper, was achieved. One of the major threats was mentioned often: the matter of corruption in government. Five days later, a high Kenyan official was arrested for corruption.

There are a lot of rich people in the world. How many of them have come by what they have gained in an honest and ethical way?

One leader from the south of Sudan, James Wani Iga, made a strong statement: "500 billion dollars disappears into private pockets in the world because of corruption." He went on to say, "To our shame, 480 billion of that is in Africa!" He made it clear that corruption was not welcome in the New Sudan. Another Sudanese leader, well known for his corruption, clapped his hands in agreement.

Later, as speaker of the legislative assembly of the government of Southern Sudan, James Wani Iga invited me to speak on "Integrity versus Corruption in Government."

It is an unfortunate fact that, when a person rises to a position of power and authority, not only in Africa, but anywhere, the chance to siphon off a chunk for selfish gain appears again and again.

Often words and deeds disagree, even in the little things with the common man on the street. It is a matter of decisions which come out of our character.

I have occasionally faltered in similar matters. And so, no doubt, have you. Unfortunately, it happens in all levels of society. "Dishonest gain" is mentioned in the Bible to have been practised by Samuel's own sons and the princes of Israel, and in the New Testament, pastors and bishops are warned to turn aside from dishonest gain.

It's not just the big guys who need to take heed—we all do. One day we will all be called to account. Better to miss the big chance than to miss God's pleasure.

18 Snow Job

The most beautiful snow scene I had ever seen greeted me one morning in late February.

There had been a gentle, but slightly wet snow falling all night and every branch, wire, ornament and surface was piled several inches high on that windless morning. My wife, Mary, asked, "Have you taken any pictures yet?" I had answered, "No." What I had done was use the snow-blower to allow life to go forward, out our driveway.

Snow is beautiful yet it covers everything. Even when I used the snow-blower little bits of pine needles and leaf parts went flying, always seeming to land on top of the blown snow. Of course all it takes is a little more snow from God's graceful clouds and it's all covered up again.

I'm certain that's where the term "snow job" originated. Snow covers a lot of things.

Take a pile of ploughed snow for instance. When the sun shines the shadowed part of the pile is still pristine white. The side revealed to the sun is dirty and grey and has everything from rags, pop cans and bits of junk. By comparison with the sunned side it looks almost black in large patches.

It's really quite similar to human life. Life throws a lot of dirt at us. Some of that stuff sticks to us, and in some cases we don't mind at all. We know right from wrong. We know the difference between righteousness and sin. But for the benefit of those who look at us, and perhaps even admire us, we do a snow job and cover it up the dirt in our own lives.

Home in Canada to date

There's an interesting, and perhaps terrifying day coming for all of us. In Psalm 44:21 we read: *"Would not God search this out? For He knows the secrets of the heart."* Also read Mark 4:22.

On the other hand, if we let God let His Light shine on us NOW, we can deal with it in this life. We can be forgiven by faith in Jesus, who died for those very sins which are hidden. Then, living in God's grace, we can deal with the everyday dirt and stand before Him cleansed and purified. The fact of the matter is: we all need a revelation from God (or simply our own knowledge of ourselves) and a daily cleansing by His penetrating light and love.

God is not deceived by the best snow job in the world. He knows us!

19 Control

I have seen many rhinoceros in Africa. I have driven my car too close to them. In fact I had to crawl under my car to fix some gear levers while a rhino glowered at me less than 50 feet away. Mary sat in the car petrified. I was not too confident myself. I had seen what a rhino can do to a car. One had charged a Volkswagen and a picture was taken of the rhino running across the plains with the Volkswagen's door firmly lodge on its horn.

I don't like to mix with wild beasts. Yet one day Mary and I stopped our car in wonder. We saw a game warden casually walking with a rhino following along behind him as a dog would on a leash. It was an unbelievable sight. But it did support what James said in chapter 3:7: *"For every kind of beast and bird, of reptile and creature of the sea, is tamed and has been tamed by mankind."* We got out and actually put our hands on the placid beast.

I never thought I'd see such a day. It was almost similar to the day I saw a 10-12 foot python in a Tim Hortons parking lot wrapped around a woman who apparently kept it as a pet. That's just not my sort of thing.

Kenya wildlife

It is true. Animals can be tamed, trained and ruled by humankind. Yet there seems to be one little beast that is quite beyond control. You'll have to read James 3:1-12 to get the full picture.

The tongue! A brutal little beast! It's harder to control than a viper and often quite as poisonous. A person's reputation can be ruined by a tongue that is false. Our words all too often rush out of our mouth before our mind fully analyses the impact, the pain and the suffering a few poorly chosen words can cause.

James 3:6 says the tongue can defile the whole body. That means the body to which it is attached. Words are powerful for good or for evil. There are times when it is best to bite your tongue hard rather than bring ruin on yourself or others.

The best control of the tongue is to turn it over to the Holy Spirit, speaking in psalms and hymns and spiritual songs, making melody rather than mayhem.

20 Truth

Javan Kavai seemed to be a nice fellow. I hired him to be the driver and salesman with the Evangel Book Mobile, which belonged to Evangel Publishing House of which I was the general manager. His job was to drive to markets and towns, open the back display of Christian books and sell books. Various languages were available. The prices were comparatively low.

When Javan returned each day the books were inventoried and the cash turned in. Too often the accounting was out. Some of the books might have been taken when Javan was not looking, but it began to add up to much more than could be accounted for in that way. I had to dismiss him from his job.

A month or so later Javan came into my office trembling and with an ashen face. The story tumbled out of him in a jumble of words and statements.

Evangel Publishing House in Kenya

He had been sitting in the back seat of a bus on the way to Nairobi when the bus had a head-on collision with a truck carrying aviation fuel. The explosion that resulted blew him right out of the emergency window at the back of the bus, hurtling him on the road. He got up and didn't stop running for about two miles he said. He thinks he was the only survivor of that crash. Everyone on the bus was incinerated in the bus, charred beyond recognition.

He came to confess the truth to me. God had spared his life. It's amazing how contact with death or suddenly facing God can turn the mind to truth and a willingness to acknowledge the truth.

After Jesus said to Pilate that He had come to bring the truth, Pilate asked, "What is truth?" Without waiting for an answer from Jesus, Pilate turned to the accusing Jews and said he found no fault in Jesus (John 18:38). Only a short time before Jesus had said, *"I am...the truth"* (John 14:6).

Do Christians lie? Yes, many do! It's different when a person is walking with God in an intimate and genuine relationship. Truth surfaces more readily. God is a God of truth and desires truth from all of us (Psalm 51:6).

And that's the truth!

21 No Deals With God

It is intriguing what a person will do or say to try to "twist" God's arm to make a deal with Him.

We've all heard stories out of various wars when a soldier in the trenches cried out in terror and desperation, "God, if you get me out of this I'll..." or "Oh God! Take away my pain and I'll...."

It's not surprising that the great majority survive their immediate danger and forget their "promise" to God. Some remember for a while. Others think of it as merely an emotional outburst and forget it.

Jesus told the parable of a man who went out to sow seed to get a harvest. Seed fell on various places and types of soil. Some seed produced little. Others produced a lot. In Deuteronomy 10:17 we are told that God is Sovereign. He needs no one's word, promise or deal. He may well bring a person to a place of remembrance of such a promise, but He was not a part of the "deal." God hears it but has no obligation to act on it. He leaves the promise part of it entirely to the person's own choice. Always has! Always will!

It depends on the character of the supplicant or the "deal maker." People of good character keep their word no matter what. Good character is built into a person by parents, circumstances, society's highest values and an understanding of ethics, integrity and right and wrong. It develops. Good character is not natural to anyone. In many cases it is a direct and immediate result of being "born again" in the sense which Jesus spoke. Old things pass away; all things become new.

Character is a continuous process of growing up in God. And that is inevitably and inextricably tied to a continuous nourishing on the Word of God. Without strong biblical input into life, character deteriorates and begins to accept the world's view of ethical and moral matters. In case you are wondering, just look at what has crept into churches in recent years. Look at the downward spiral of society in general!

We are God's subjects and servants. Even though He sent His Son Jesus Christ to be servant and sacrifice for man and his needs, God is not at our beck and call. You can't make deals with a sovereign God.

Yet we can and may call on Him in our time of distress and need. Out of pure mercy and grace He will hear us and answer—even though He doesn't have to. *"For the LORD your God is God of gods and LORD of lords, the great God, mighty and awesome, who shows no partiality nor takes a bribe"* (Deuteronomy 10:17).

22 Hope

During our time in East Africa as missionaries, my wife, Mary, and I moved about like nomads. We seldom stayed in the same house for more than a year or so. We lived in 17 different houses in the 17 years we live there. With every move we hoped this would be the last. We really wanted to settle in a little more permanently. It never happened. But we never lost hope.

When we finally came back to Canada in 1979, it seemed to start all over again. First in a rented apartment on the 30th floor! Then we moved into a semi-detached house, which we bought without enough money for a down payment—so we borrowed. That lasted a while but it also ended. Yet it ended with a bang. In nine years inflation had raised the value more than four times the original price. We moved out to the country outside Brantford, Ontario, where we eventually paid off the mortgage and have been ever since—more than 22 years now. We sometimes think it is a bit like heaven—finally a permanent home!

50th wedding anniversary

For more than 35 years and too many moves to want to remember, we never lost hope that we would one day have a place which was actually our own. It's possible we could move again. Our children may have to pick the residence. But even beyond that there is one more final move.

This is one of the great blessings of being a Christian. In Colossians 1:5 we read of *"the hope which is laid up for you in heaven."* And in Romans 5:1-2 Paul talks about how our faith will triumph in times of trouble, and that we can *"rejoice in hope of the glory of God."*

Meanwhile we are on earth surrounded by a very depraved society which has turned its back on God and against those of us who speak too openly and frankly about our faith in Christ. We are "old-fashioned" and "un-cool." We cling to purportedly outdated moral standards. Such pressure is put on Christians nowadays that it seems a shameful thing to be a Christian in the eyes of the "unwashed" (in the blood) masses.

King David knew where to get his strength in such times. He wrote in Psalm 119:116, *"Uphold me according to Your word, that I may live; And do not let me be ashamed of my hope."*

And in spite of it all, and according to Philippians 1:20, like Paul we need not be ashamed of our bold stand for Jesus Christ. I *hope* you really understand that!

23 Humility

I'm sure you've heard of the author who wrote the book *Humility, and How I Achieved It.* The book had a full life-size picture of himself which unfolded from the front of the book. The story is apocryphal of course, but it does illustrate a point. Humility is not something about which to be proud. It is something to pursue.

Humility is primarily a clear recognition and acknowledgement of God as sovereign. To really know God is a humbling experience.

The Old Testament is replete with exhortations, cautions and mentions of people who ruined their own lives by refusing to humble themselves before God. Humility when properly practised will eventually become intrinsic to the nature of one who humbles himself. James (4:10) and Peter (1 Peter 5:6) agree on a very essential point: we are to humble ourselves. Otherwise we may be not only humbled but humiliated. Jesus made it most clear when he said in Matthew 23:12, *"And whoever exalts himself will be humbled, and he who humbles himself will be exalted."*

God blesses the humble. An observation made by King Solomon in Proverbs 22:4 points out some very interesting results of genuine humility; *"By humility and the fear of the LORD Are riches and honor and life."* That is a truth for all age groups. Youth, who generally start life wanting to be well off, need only be humble before God. Middle aged folk would like to be respected and even honoured. They need only be humble before God and others. Older folk can expect a longer blessed life if they remain humble before God. Then there is the promise of wisdom to the humble (Proverbs 11:2).

Unfortunately, there are those who quietly trumpet their humility by demonstrating their deep commitment to religious affairs, their asceticism and self-denial. This is fleshly and has no value before God. Colossians 2:23 says: *"These things indeed have an appearance of wisdom in self-imposed religion, false humility, and neglect of the body, but are of no value against the indulgence of the flesh."*

True humility is submitting to God in all things, public and private, considering others more important than one's self.

24 Terror Is Optional

When I first read the intercepted letter which was forwarded to me by the RCMP and written from an El Qaida cell in Montreal to the Islamist president of Sudan calling for my "elimination," it was somewhat disconcerting. It was written in Arabic with the English in between the lines. I asked my friend Nizar Shaheen to provide a second translation for me so that I could be sure I was really under threat of death.

Apparently, I deserved to die for my revealing the terrible violations of human rights against the people of southern Sudan by the northern Islamist extremists.

At that point I could have decided to back off and go into hiding under my bed.

I'm not built that way. Perhaps I should say "I'm not re-built" that way. When I decided to follow Jesus, obey His call on my life and truly accept Him as LORD of my life, I knew the risks I was taking. I had long before concluded that my obedience to Christ must necessarily involve some personal inconvenience, some discomfort, some sacrifice and some risk.

I choose not to be terrorized. Fear does not come from God. Terror is satanic at its source. I will not be afraid of the terror by night or the arrow by day. Proverbs 3:25 is assuring and worth obeying. My life cannot and will not be dictated by threats of death and terror.

The lazy man stays in his house, perhaps getting up to peek out the window from time to time, because he says there might be a lion in the streets (Proverbs 22:13). The called of God can be neither lazy nor fearful. He or she puts on the whole armor of God and gets on with the job.

Rather, *"knowing, therefore, the terror of the Lord, we persuade men,"* Paul said (2 Corinthians 5:11).

I'm more concerned with the day I face God than I am about either the threats or actions of mere men. And with that settled it is much easier to sleep at night—on top of the bed!

25 Sacrifice?

I have had the same thing said to me many times by people who don't quite understand God and His call on a person's life. It usually goes something like this, "Cal, what you are doing for God around the world is such a sacrifice! I just don't know how you can do it!" My normal answer sounds rather bland, but it is what I believe: "What I do involves little or no sacrifice. I am just being obedient to what God has called me to do."

When I was part of a group of people who were ambushed in Sudan by bandits, it was to some a harrowing experience. Not to me. I just disregarded the guns pointed at me and began demanding back what was being taken from us. I didn't even think that I might be "sacrificing" my life in that situation. I simply obeyed an inner impulse to demand the return of what had already been taken. On the surface, it seemed like a stupid thing to do. I think the bandits were more disturbed by what I did than we were by what they did.

Later, when they were caught, I had a chance to tell them of God's love and forgiveness, and to ask for clemency for them. As the law stood at that time, robbery, rape and murder were punishable by death in front of a firing squad. The law said one thing; the Lord said another.

But sacrifice is hardly an understood concept in our society. It seems a sacrifice when someone surrenders a parking place to someone else. That's not sacrifice: that's common courtesy. It's not a sacrifice to give to the poor. We are usually giving out of our comparative abundance.

God is much more interested in our doing the right thing than the "sacrificing" of our rights to someone else's demands or needs. Read 1 Corinthians 6 for the biblical view.

CCCI missions staff

"I'll have my rights," yells the carnal mind. The spiritual mind submits to the Word, which exhorts us to suffer the spoiling of our goods with equanimity, to turn the other cheek, to be righteous without trespassing on justice. If that's a sacrifice, get over it!

Proverbs 21:3 says: *"To do righteousness and justice Is more acceptable to the LORD than sacrifice."*

26 The Right Church
(Mine, of Course!)

I have been in 75 countries, and many, many more churches than I could count.

I've studied theology and believe we must know theology. I've studied the Bible and believe we must know and believe the Bible. I was raised in my own denomination and believe in its statement of faith. I have read discourses on dozens of biblical topics and heard hundreds of sermons by people from my own denomination.

But there's a problem: I don't always agree with them.

Then, of course, there are other denominations. Some I have major problems with; others I find quite acceptable. Yet I can and do work in unity with the whole spectre of Christian denominations—for one reason and one reason alone: If they confess that Jesus Christ is God's Son and that He is the only Saviour for humankind, then I can fit in.

No one church has a perfect doctrinal structure. No one denomination has a corner on biblical truth, no matter how loud and far they trumpet that claim. Theological discussions and arguments have existed since forever. And they should continue. It's always good to discuss the Bible. But I have to also say, it's even better to obey and live by it!

People can be incredibly pig-headed about some of their beliefs. I think the apostle Paul was rather obstinate in his beliefs. But it was the apostle Paul who wrote: *"For now we see through a glass, darkly; but then face to face: now I know in part; but then shall I know even as also I am known"* (1Corinthians 13:12 KJV).

Do you get it? My church is right in most things, and so is yours. But our eyes will finally know how terribly wrong we have been in some areas of our beliefs and even our convictions. Yet in spite of our differences and our arguments and divisions, Jesus said, *"I will build my church, and the gates of hell shall not prevail against it"* (Matthew 16:18, ESV).

Better to be involved in the building than in the super-defining of the church!

I can hardly wait for heaven.

27 Know When to Run!

The first time I really had to run was when we met an elephant while innocently walking down a road in Uganda. The second time, in Kenya, it wasn't quite as innocent.

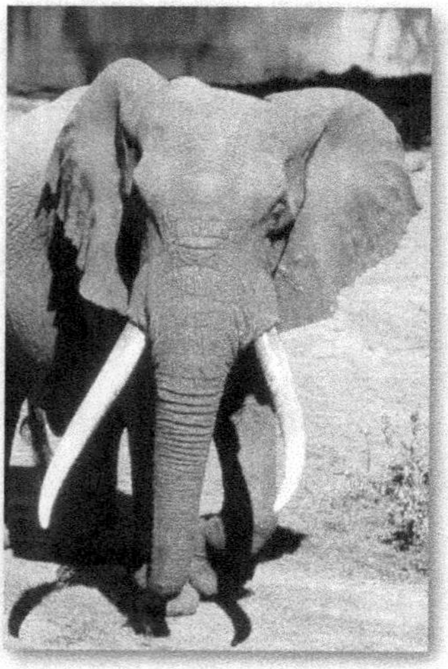

I was hunting for meat for our larder and had carefully followed an Impala buck on foot into some bush on the Loita plains. I came out considerably faster when I had a rhino suddenly charge me. My small 30.06 gun was no match for a rhino. I made safety as you may have noticed, since I'm writing about it. Had the eyesight of elephants and rhinos been somewhat better than it

is, someone else might have been writing this account.

Pick your flights. Know when to run—away—fast! Otherwise, you may be a casualty.

One of the greatest mistakes many Christians make is the assumption that we can flirt with dangerous practices or associations with the "confidence" that we can get away with it before the trap snaps.

Cheese is not a natural food for mice. They don't have any idea how to make it. But how many mice have been trapped by something which is not their regular fare?

For Christians, there are certain "rules" which keep us from spiritual calamity. The Bible teaches us all of them. Most of them are also written by the Spirit of God on our hearts. *"Abstain from all appearance of evil"* (1 Thessalonians 5:22 KJV), for instance. Proverbs 4:14-17 adds a few more wise instructions.

Pick your flights. Know when to run—away—fast! Otherwise, you may be a casualty.

King David, the beloved of God, got himself involved in adultery and murder because he didn't know when to run—away—fast.

Addictions and traps will not fasten onto you if your first step is away, rather than naively toward a danger you assume is "contained" and therefore not threatening.

I've done some running in my time, and it was toward my Refuge.

28 Liar

While living in Kenya, I received a long cardboard tube in the mail. When I opened it, I was surprised to find a beautiful Diploma with my name beautifully inscribed on it. It stated that "Calvin Richard Bombay is hereby granted this honorary Doctorate in Literature." It was as surprise. I felt honoured. I wondered where it came from and why!

I had many thoughts. Perhaps it was because I had been working in Christian literature for years in Kenya. Perhaps it was because I was president of the Evangelical Literature Fellowship of East Africa, including Kenya, Uganda and what was Tanganyika (now Tanzania, including Zanzibar). Or perhaps it was granted because I had written several books.

It was granted by the "London Institute of Applied Research" in England. I made inquiries. I framed it and hung it on my office wall. I looked at it, pleased...at first. Then, I suddenly had a flash of insight. As I looked at the granting institute, "London Institute of Applied Research," I suddenly realized that the acronym spelled out the word "LIAR." Someone had probably spent all of $10.00, or even $25.00 for this elaborate joke. I laughed myself silly for a while then realized there was something to learn here.

Jesus said in Luke 6:26, *"Woe to you when all men speak well of you."* When I read the rest of that verse, I thought I might be on someone's "kill" list.

Then I thought of the Scriptural warning that we should not think more highly of ourselves that we should. In that way, I'd be putting myself on my own kill list. Pride comes before destruction, and a haughty spirit before a fall.

I still have it on my office wall. Humour is a great way to become comfortable with visitors.

We all need to be careful not to believe all the wonderful things people say about us.

The only time I ever walked on water was when the pond was frozen!

29 Life's Three Stages

Don't you wish that we were all as wise a Solomon? We're not. At least I am clearly not. Obviously I could never have written with the wisdom of Solomon. Oh yes, I occasionally have a flash of wisdom. It's not too long afterward when I realize again I have an enormous lack of wisdom.

Life is made up of stages. They overlap to a degree and you normally have to get through one before you can get to the other. Youth, middle age and then "old!" I'm just guessing, but I wonder if Solomon had those three stages in mind when he wrote: *"By humility and the fear of the LORD Are riches and honor and life"* (Proverbs 22:4).

Have you ever noticed that younger folk seem more interested in making money and getting rich? They have plans, things they want to get—a comfortable life, secure retirement. Quite legitimate! Most people can relate to that. But not all people have the opportunity to prepare for a productive and happy life of work, relaxation and occasional holidays. Poverty annuls that possibility for millions.

There is this thing called middle-age. I'm not quite sure when it begins or ends. I'm guessing that I may be past that at 71, though there are time when both my mind and body claim otherwise. In that stage, people generally want to be well thought of and honoured, and some even want to be revered. Honour does not always come with position or authority. Money cannot buy true honour. In Proverbs 15:33 we read: *"before honor is humility."*

You have also probably noticed how the older people get, the more concerned they become about their health. Often they get on to food fads which promise better health, weight control and longer life. Some work—a bit. Others are scams. There is no doubt that a healthy lifestyle as well as a well-balanced diet can improve our lifespan. Of course life has no guarantees against accidents and death by disaster catching many of us.

But the Word of God is right and true. Proverbs 22:4 is true. *"By humility and the fear of the LORD Are riches and honor and life."* This is a great foundation for sensible living.

True humility is a great antidote to poverty, disrespect and early death.

30 Self-Control

Actually, I saw it coming, but not in the form and filthiness in which it was delivered.

I was walking down Yonge Street in Toronto on a very wide section of sidewalk in front of the former Eaton's department store. I was going north. "He" was coming south. About 20 feet from me. His eyes locked on mine with a burning hatred. I had never seen the man before. He had probably recognized me from my daily appearances on television.

He wove his way through the northbound pedestrians with his eyes locked on me. As he came up to me with hostile eyes he spat a great gob of sputum and whatever else he had hocked up, which spewed right down the front of me. A woman exclaimed in shock beside me.

My immediate and first reaction was to fold my right fist and deck him. After all, I had done some boxing in my younger days. But something else took over in an instant. Self-control! Looking back at the situation and remembering the reaction of several people around me at the time, I wondered at the transformation of my mind and my own reaction. I did nothing but hesitate, take out my handkerchief and wipe it off.

I can only conclude that he had seen what I stand for as a Christian on television and had a very violent disagreement with my faith and views.

On the other hand, I can also only conclude that one of the fruits of the Spirit had grown instantly and my reaction was Christian (Galatians 5:22-23). I was about to whack him on the first cheek before he even had a chance to turn the other. But the Spirit of God produced an instant fruit of His Spirit.

This sort of thing should not be unexpected in a society which has less and less respect for God and His claims on our lives. All you have to do is read Matthew 5:1-12 (note verses 10-11).

If you live right, some people will simply not treat you right.

Giving a commentary on 100 Huntley Street

31 Dishonest Gain

In the late 1990s I was involved in "redeeming slaves" from northern Sudan, where they had been taken as captive by the Islamist raiders who robbed, raped and pillaged the villagers in the south of Sudan.

We had to change from American dollars to one of the several currencies used locally in Sudan. That could be Sudanese pounds, which were not even current, or dinars. Even Kenyan and Ugandan shillings were used in the south.

The paper currency was so long in circulation that it became filthy and greasy. Often, the only way we knew its value was the size compared to other bills. Almost every time I handled those dirty bills, the term "filthy lucre" came to mind. That's an old

Negotiations with slave retrievers, 1998

"King James" term for dishonest gain.

We were buying slaves out of unspeakable conditions and restoring them back to home and families in the south. Those slave owners had a motive: make money. We too had a motive: free people who are in bondage. But then fraud entered into it and some people made dishonest gain by "freeing" people who were never ever real slaves.

We often dipped into our own pockets at the last moment to "free one more slave" when they were genuine. Every dollar was accounted for. There's a moral here: don't mess with God's money.

Unfortunately, I know of an all-too-common and unhealthy parallel here in North America. It is not a new phenomenon. You can find some reference to similar acts in 1 Samuel 2:29, where Eli's sons were in the priesthood and took advantage of it *"to make* [themselves] *fat with the best."* It makes me think of Proverbs 1:19 and Ezekiel 22:27. Character and integrity don't always have the upper hand in all humanity.

More recently, there are people who are in Christian ministry with wrong underlying motives. The extravagant lifestyles of some Christian leaders illustrate this. You need to read Titus 1:10-11 to get the picture.

It is possible to abuse God's grace by turning from honest ministry to the pursuit of riches while in ministry. Then it may be asked, "Why do we still see miracles in the ministry of such people?"

The answer is simple: God still honours His Word when it is preached, but one who abuses his position of spiritual leadership will one day face God on the issue. It is faith in Jesus Christ which changes lives, not faith in any preacher, no matter how famous he or she may be.

Godliness is great gain! This is true especially when it has contentment with it (1 Timothy 6:6).

32 A Massive Problem

I woke up with a start! There seemed to be a lot of confusion and loud grunting noises outside the tent, which was shaking. Jim Hooten, a Southern Baptist missionary, whispered across the tent to me, "I think there are elephants out there!" We were camping in the bush in Uganda, near Murchison Falls.

We crept over to the zippered door, opened the bottom and stuck our heads out. Elephants! A mother and baby! Uh oh! That could be dangerous. A tent rope was mixed with the grass the mother was grazing, causing the tent to shimmy around us. Mother elephants can be very aggressively protective about their young. We retreated into the tent. Scared? Absolutely! Terrified? Well, somehow being shaken around trapped in a big bag of tent didn't appeal.

We had no weapon big enough to handle an elephant. And yet. . .

As strange as it may seem, we drove that big mama away with a flashlight. We kept flashing it on and off and across her eyes. She just kept backing up, over bushes and small trees, until she was gone, baby and all.

Light is a powerful elemental ingredient of the world around us. Light is always good for you.

Darkness is always equated with bad things. Kids imagine monsters in the dark. Slugs and crawly things live in the dark. Things people would be ashamed to do in the light are done in the dark. Light exposes. Light reveals not just to the naked eye but to the spiritual eye. Jesus spoke about this in John 3:19-21.

God made the light for good and for us. Just as a little light like a flashlight can drive away an elephant, the light of God, Jesus Christ in me, can drive away the dark forces which threaten me. We can all have victory as the light of God both exposes and dispels evil. It's a relationship thing.

Walk in it! Let it shine.

33 Influence

"Why did you steal his iPod?"

"The devil made me do it!" he answered.

Quite frankly the devil gets more credit than he deserves.

Every one of us has the power to choose what, where, when, how and why we do things. The only thing the devil invented was rebellion—against God and His desire for our association.

Right and wrong are being continually redefined by almost every society. With cannibals it was right to eat your enemy. That's changed. As I write, laws are being constructed to change what was once wrong to now be right, in the eyes of human law. Sociopaths are the result of some sort of influence. Parents, trauma, society, repetitive advertising: they all have their affect. Something or someone influences all of us.

On the other hand, every single one of us has influence. It may not be on the rich and powerful, but certainly we influence others both by our words and our actions and our lack of words or actions. We make impressions on people for good or for bad. If we repeat that influence enough, those we influence come around to our way of thinking and being. Eli's two sons, in 1 Samuel 2:24, were told, *"**You** make the LORD's people transgress"* (emphasis added).

Influence on others is inevitable. You have influence on both the weak and the strong. Be careful that you don't unwittingly twist the arms of the weak behind their backs until they succumb, bowing to opinions and actions which are yours and yours alone. You may cause someone to flounder through your own misguided behaviour.

No one should be made to "transgress against the Lord."

That's devilish in the end, but it remains your influence.

34 Go!

For almost seventeen years in Africa I did not contract malaria. For two years I took prophylactics but the bad taste finally put me off. For fifteen years I took nothing. Three weeks before finally coming home to Canada, I got malaria—bad! I felt like doing nothing but groan and complain. I didn't know whether I wanted to die or get better.

Only very rarely have I ever felt that thing called lassitude. Malaria did it. Even when I have a bad cold I still go to work. I have found that things don't get done unless you do them. That first step has to be taken. I don't like cleaning out my chicken coop, but it won't be done by the chickens. Just the opposite in fact.

I'm not necessarily the first off the starting block, but I'm always in the race. I wake up ready and raring to go.

I sometimes get myself into a bit of trouble because I start in at something I'm not quite ready to do. Either the timing is bad or I'm just in too much of a hurry. Side trips when I am driving to a specific destination don't appeal to me. I'd rather be very early than a little late.

There are times when only one step forward changes all the conditions which stand in the way of progress. Standing in front of an

Mary and Cal

automatic door for a month will not open the door. Step forward one step and a whole store full of wonderful things is opened to you.

I can relate to Peter when he was in prison while a whole house full of people was praying for him. An angel gave him the boot, and he awakened to a whole new experience, and as he walked out of that prison, the iron gates swinging wide by themselves. But it all started with his first obedient step at the instructions of the angel. How different it could have been had he been unbelieving or waiting for legal authority. It did seem too good to be true but even in his possible hesitation he moved forward.

Occasionally we must be still and know that God is God. But more often than not, God is telling us to get up off our duffs and get on the move. Remember it is the "steps" of a good man that are ordered of the Lord (Psalm 37:23), not the quantum leaps.

The first single step toward the closed but automatically opening door is what sets it all in motion. That's leadership. Others will follow.

Just be sure you're moving through the right door for the right reasons at the right time.

35 The Name

When Jesus walked the earth, the name of Jesus was as common as any other. James, John and Matthew were just as common. The name Jesus appears twenty-three times in the writings of the Jewish historian Josephus. Only two of those mentioned refer to Jesus of Nazareth of the New Testament.

Jesus is still a common name on the tongues of blasphemous people. His name is often less used by those who know Him as Lord and Saviour.

After Jesus' resurrection, Peter preached in the name of Jesus Christ. The lame man at the temple was healed in the name of Jesus Christ. When Jerusalem was buzzing with the marvellous power of the name of Jesus, the leaders of the Jews called the disciples before them and gave harsh warning against the use of the name "Jesus" in their preaching and teaching.

The term *God* had specific meaning in the minds of the Jews—Jehovah, the Creator, the Almighty Sovereign God. But today, the term God has become almost generic and is a tool in the mouths of those who would like to play down the name and role of the Christ, Jesus of Nazareth. *God* can refer to the "deity' or multiplicity of "deities' of any religion or cult.

The disciples were reprimanded a second time for preaching in the name of Jesus. It was the name of Jesus which was the sore point with the religious elite. The disciples' answer was straight and to the point. We will obey God rather than man. And when they said "God" they meant the God and Father of our Lord Jesus Christ and Jesus Himself!

While it is absolutely true that Jesus of Nazareth who was raised from the dead is in every respect God come in the flesh, all too often we as Christians back off from the name Jesus as being too specific and use "God" to soften our testimony and accommodate the mindset of our present society.

If we are to make an impact on our world and if we are to lead people into a relationship with God, it is the irreplaceable name of Jesus that we must talk about. In Acts 4, we read of the centrality of the name Jesus. Verse 12 states it most clearly: *"Nor is there salvation in any other, for there is* ***no other name under heaven given among men by which we must be saved****"* (emphasis added).

Jesus is the Christ of God. There is no other name. Never be ashamed to name Jesus as your God and Saviour.

There is no other!

36 Faithfulness

My wife and I have a formerly Muslim friend whom we led to the Lord through friendship and witnessing about Jesus. She owned a very fine restaurant serving excellent Indian cuisine. In an attempt to be accommodating she hired some non-Indian waitresses. They appeared to be very fine people, congenial, and seemed to be doing their jobs well.

It was some time before a discrepancy appeared to our friend. More food was being served than seemed to be paid for at the end of each day. A closer watch revealed that these waitresses were picking up bills which some diners left on their tables, and when another similar order was made, the same bill was presented again, paid for, and the money pocketed by these unfaithful waitresses. They were of course dismissed. Their salaries or rewards were cut off. No chance for them to find a higher, more trusted position.

The owner of the restaurant, having been burned once, decided that only members of her own family would serve the tables and handle the money.

It's not for nothing that Paul wrote in 1 Corinthians 4:2: *"Moreover it is required in stewards that one be found faithful."*

I looked up the word "faithfulness" in the Bible. The word is used only 27 times (NKJV). Twenty-two of those times it talks of the unfaltering faithfulness of God. The four other uses of the word are used in the oft dubious faithfulness of men. Look at Psalm 119:90 as an instance of God's faithfulness. By comparison, look at Proverbs 20:6, Matthew 25:21, and finally 2 Timothy 2:13: *"If we are faithless, He remains faithful; He cannot deny Himself."*

It is also important to note that one of the fruit of the Spirit is faithfulness. As members of God's family we should be exhibiting that very important fruit in our everyday living as Christians. And being faithful in small things leads to the opportunity to be faithful in larger things.

Is it any wonder God cuts some people off from His blessings? As a result they do not experience much advance, if any, in their relationship with God and the rest of His family.

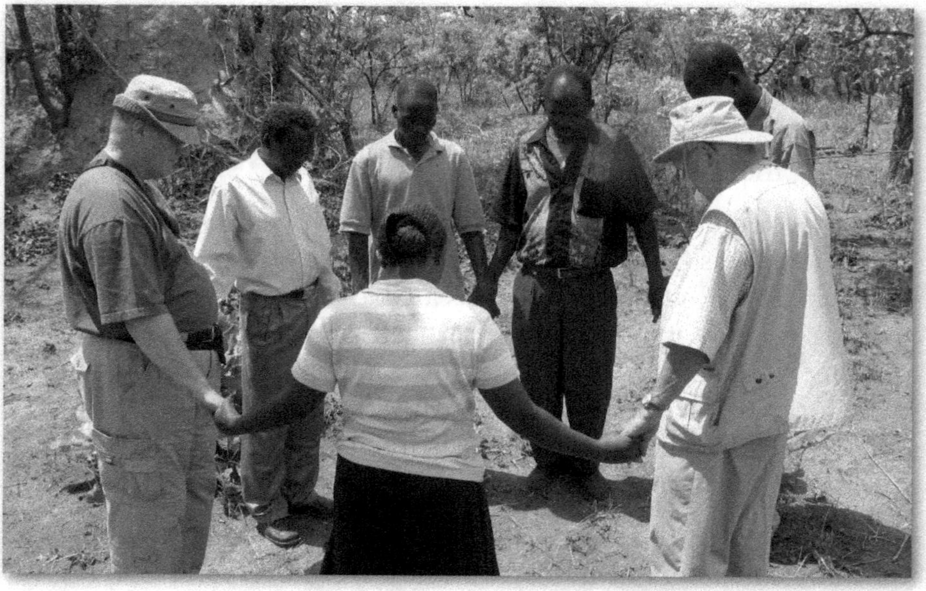

Launch of first 2,000 acre farm, Sudan

37 Goals

"Where ya goin'?" he asked.

"Sudan," I answered.

"You're crazy!" he said.

At that point I'd had enough. I told him I was going to Sudan to free men, women and children from extremely abusive slavery in the north of Sudan. I explained the whole horror of the reality of what was happening to the black and predominantly Christian south of Sudan at the hands of extreme Islamists who had tens of thousands of slaves for free labour and free sex who were expendable—at a price. I had a goal back then in 1996. The slave redemption process became corrupt but I still have goals in Sudan: Large farms for large crops for the millions of voiceless people dying of hunger.

I've had goals before, and I have other goals as well, even though some claim retirement is a great thing. Life seems rather pointless without goals. I suppose I could lie back and relax, use the remote to turn me into a zombie and die in a year or so. But I have goals. It's the Christian way!

My life is driven with purpose. The apostle Paul speaks of the past, the present and its future in Philippians 3:13-14: "*Brethren, I do not count myself to have apprehended; but one thing I do, forgetting those things which are behind and reaching forward to those things which are ahead, I press toward the goal for the prize of the upward call of God in Christ Jesus.*"

Those last three words are the secret of life and happiness: "*in Christ Jesus.*" If your life is hid with Christ in God, then between now and the assurance of our eternal goal, we have obligations under God to fit into God's plan to change the world.

Jesus' goal was to come into the world to save sinners. If the last few verses of the Gospel of Mark mean anything at all, they mean we have the same goal as Jesus, and we are under His command.

Pursue your goals. You'll live longer and enjoy life much more. Life without purpose is blah!

38 High Thinking

Envy is not a nice trait, but I must admit there are times when I am envious of another person's intellect and their ability to think through a situation and express themselves clearly. The Christian apologist Ravi Zacharias is one such person. Malcolm Muggeridge was another.

Is that such a bad thing?

On the other hand, there are some folk who take very little time to simply sit and think, reflect, observe and analyze their own lives and circumstances. Fewer still try to take on the lofty philosophical questions which might just take a fleeting squirt through their minds.

Intelligence and rational thought are something to be pursued. Every human being has enough intelligence to give time to think and at least cogitate on some probing questions. Yet in recent years we have succumbed to the mass media and let the few who appear on television do our thinking for us. They form our opinions for us. We become almost brainwashed into being sheep without shepherds. We hear everything in public media with a strong but most often biased opinion. Whoever convinced us that we are not allowed to have our own biases?

Perhaps we should take more time, slow down life to a degree and think more in-depth about our lives and circumstances and the affect we have on other people. We are allowed to think, you know! We are allowed to have opinions, convictions and questions about life.

Perhaps the one area where we do think, perhaps even more than we should, is about ourselves. Where do we fit into the general scheme of things? How high up the social ladder do we consider ourselves? Are our opinions, convictions and biases more valid than others?

Being rational about ourselves is much more difficult than being rational about others. Assessing ourselves is a little more dangerous than it may seem. All of us have a tendency to think we are more "right" than most, if not all others. That's when pride can lift its ugly head.

The apostle Paul made the statement in Romans 12:3 that we are *"not to think of [ourselves] more highly than [we] ought to think, but to think soberly."*

And it's also a good thing to keep ourselves from thinking too highly of others. Idol worship is encouraged in this day and age, but it is deceptive. Peter, in Acts 10:26, addresses this.

Think! Think all you want! But think soberly. Think right. The Scriptures can help you in that area.

Giving a commentary on 100 Huntley Street

39 Think Before You Shrink

Computers are really quite a wonderful electronic marvel. I write with them, transmit immediate mail to friends and associates worldwide, and research any subject I choose. It's great. I'm not too sure how I could ever get as much done as I do without them. But they are also dangerous.

In a front page story in Canada's *Maclean's* magazine of June 2005, I read "How computers make our kids stupid"—rather a shocking concept to some. Simple mathematics becomes a matter of keystrokes rather than thought. The wonders of nature are replaced with microchips and gigabytes. The healthy fun and games playing outside has changed and has been replaced with the gloom in a room around a digital screen. Lots of information but little cause for thought.

It seems that our new world system is turning our minds and souls to jelly. We have entered a stage in human history when the mind has begun to shrink. This does not apply to everyone of course, but the western world has become enamoured with technology, especially if it saves us time and work. (What exactly do we save that time for?) We have more time to be mesmerized by TV series, fattened by fast foods and reduced to a social insurance number that pays taxes.

In all these advances, we are leaving behind some of the best things in life. Some of humanity's ancient wisdom is dwindling to become high-tech movies of special effects and minuscule meaning. There are some things worth saving. Solomon, an earthy but brilliant mind, wrote, *"Do not remove the ancient landmark Which your fathers have set"* (Proverbs 22:28). There are certain foundations in human history and relationships with which we should not tamper.

Solomon also said that we should avoid people who are bent on changing everything and anything (Proverbs 24:21).

I'll never throw my computer away. Yet at the same time, I'll never abandon the simple mind-and-soul-resting activity of growing my own vegetables, lying on my back on a starlit night and looking at the bigger picture...or just sitting and thinking.

40 Goodness

As we were looking down into the coffin, a man nearby said, "He was a good man." Several people were startled. Everyone in the funeral parlour knew the man as a rough, rowdy foul-tongued man who was abusive to everyone with whom he had contact. He was in trouble with the police and had been in and out of jail and had no use for the Church, much less God.

There was a creeping silence. People knew it was not true. The thought passed through my mind, "Is this an attempt to try to elevate him into to some sort of sainthood just in case he had a chance with God after death?"

Goodness cannot be assigned. You either have it or you don't. A few Scriptures passed through my mind such as Romans 2:4, which refers to God's judgment: "*Or do you despise the riches of His goodness, forbearance, and longsuffering, not knowing that the goodness of God leads you to repentance?*" And that's where goodness starts in people: repentance.

The Bible says there is none good but God. In Psalm 107:8, we are encouraged to give thanks for God's goodness. Without God's goodness, we'd all be fried.

As it says in Proverbs 20:6 most men like to think of themselves as good. We are to reflect God's goodness by doing good things. That's according to Jesus in Matthew 5:16. That brings glory to God. In 1 Peter 2:15, we are told that we can actually shut the mouths of foolish and ignorant people by simply doing good. Good is a gift of the Spirit but it comes from Him not from us.

Of course we can have a good reputation but where does that come from for the Christian? Acts 6:30 spells it out fairly clearly. Most of the gifts of the Spirit need to be accepted and worked on.

My goodness! You'd think it was complicated the way some people talk.

41 Peace

I heard the gunshot after I heard a snap right beside my right ear. I had just moved slightly to the left from the video camera on which I was recording a statement by Zamba Duku, managing director of the Savannah Farmers Cooperatives we had started in Sudan. It took a moment for me to realize that a bullet had just missed me. Two more gunshots rang out.

Neither Zamba nor I flinched. We just kept on recording the statement.

Sudan was not at peace at the time. The civil war between the Islamist north and the predominantly Christian south was still raging, though there was little fighting in the area around Kajokeji, where we were at the time. Land mines by the thousands were still buried on roads, paths and haphazardly in fields.

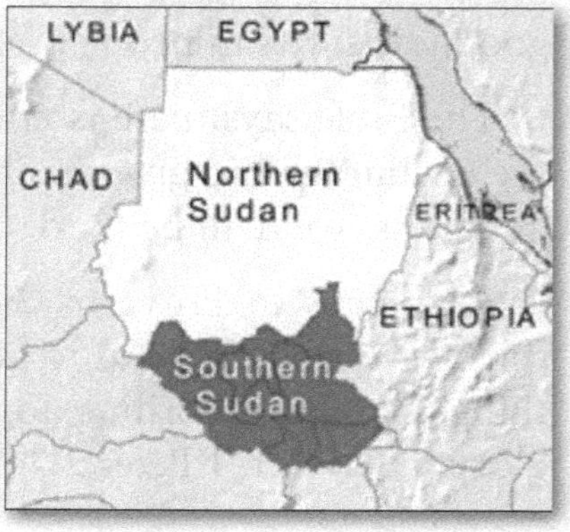

Jesus said,

"Peace I leave with you, My peace I give to you; not as the world gives do I give to you. Let not your heart be troubled, neither let it be afraid."

John 14:27

I have had many experiences, not only in Sudan, but in other parts of Africa which many would have thought to be harrowing, frightening! And it was often downright dangerous. Through it all I have never lost my peace. It may sound strange to some, but though I am a very vulnerable human being like anyone else I have a sense of deep security because of the presence of the Holy Spirit, which I acknowledge with gratitude. It's not a peace that I have to suddenly gasp and grasp to get when things get rough. It's a peace that is just "there" always.

It has nothing to do with my patience or impatience, my state of mind or circumstances. It is just a peace that is assured to any Christian who simply believes what the Bible says is true. Paul wrote in Philippians 4:7 about a peace that is beyond human understanding. The prophet Isaiah in 26:3 talks about the peace of mind that is a part of the life of someone who acknowledges God is always present.

In John 14:27, Jesus said, *"Peace I leave with you, My peace I give to you; not as the world gives do I give to you. Let not your heart be troubled, neither let it be afraid."*

There is no government agency, psychological practitioner or changed circumstance that can give this kind of peace. It is a gift of the Spirit of God. Help yourself! It's all yours for the receiving.

42 Patience

Patience does not come naturally to me. And I can prove it! I *have* proved it many times.

I lived in Africa. Matters do not move swiftly in Africa. There is lots of room for patience in Africa for anyone who doesn't know the culture. Perhaps my Nigerian experience is the best example.

I was to travel from Kenya to display the products of Evangel Publishing House to the missions, bookshops and distributors in Nigeria. Rather than pay the exorbitant price to carry heavy boxes of books by plane, I sent them in advance in a small shipment. That was my first mistake. The second mistake was thinking that I need only go to the warehouse at the airport in Lagos and pick them up.

I had a Nigerian pastor with me; otherwise it could have been much worse. The first office I went to referred me to another. That went on for 27 offices, all complete with rubber stamps and another referral. Somewhere about the 15th office I began to recognise I was being given the runaround, recognizing the same offices in this continuing loop.

The Nigerian pastor finally told me they were looking for "dash" (a bribe). My patience was razor thin. But almost to my own surprise I came out with a rational demand. "Stop expecting any money from me, since I have decided to sit here and wait all day until you release my parcel!" It worked. Patience had produced its perfect work.

Then there was the nine hour drive through a constant traffic jam into the centre of Lagos....

I have found that you have to make yourself patient. It is not a gift. It is not easy. It is not natural. It must be pursued. In

1 Timothy 6:11 we read about it. I have also found that patience can be developed only under trying circumstances (James 1:3). Paul points out that patience is normally called for during persecution, longsuffering, tribulation and endurance in rough circumstances as we wait for the coming of the God of all patience.

Patience is rarely a natural trait. Most of us still have to pursue it.

I've often wondered if there is a correlation between impatience and ulcers. I have never had an ulcer but the fact that I don't might just be on the edge of being a miracle.

43 Exploitation

There is massive difference between exploiting the natural resources of the land's resources and exploiting people who are at a disadvantage.

People who take advantage of others of lesser position or power have very serious character flaws. There are plenty of examples in the Bible that illustrate this. In Isaiah 58:3, you might find the original reason for labour unions being formed. In Malachi 3:5, it is reinforced with some reference to other evils which God will judge. 2 Peter 2:3 notes people who will twist and pervert truth in order to exploit others. Uninformed people need to be cautious! Read those verses.

Yet, even when we have positive knowledge of the right of our cause and purpose, there are times and situations which demand a second thought before we act. God has a plan, not only for the whole world, but for all of us as individuals. That plan also has a timetable. God's timetable is perfect.

Some people I have known have tried to get ahead of God at one time or another. They force the fulfilment of their vision and dream leaving wounded and exploited people all around them as they go for *their* goal. They have set their heart so much on the goal that they don't even consider the collateral damage of their ambition, even though the ambition and goal is honourable in itself. They can't seem to trust the Holy Spirit—in other people.

I once worked in a situation where such was the case. The wounded were left as discards, all sacrificed as expendable in the light of someone's "greater vision."

Between the time that David had been anointed king but not yet proclaimed as king, he had several chances to speed up the process and seize power. But he backed off, even exposing himself to real danger, rather than exploit a promising opportunity. It's recorded in 1 Samuel 21. It's worth reading. Talk about drama!

David would simply not harm God's anointed. It is God who puts one up and another down. Promotion *does* come from the Lord. It was just not in David's character to exploit an easy opportunity for personal fulfilment.

People of character put the needs and positions of others in their proper perspective.

44 Over My Dead Body

Working as a missionary on a mission station is much like living in a fishbowl. Not one of your fellow missionaries is very far out of sight even though at times one might wish it so. Missionaries, like anyone else on earth, are not as holy and perfect as many naive admirers imagine. They have faults and foibles like any other human.

There are such things as personality conflicts. Sometimes they become almost monstrous, simply because of human nature. Even of those who know, love and serve the Lord, there are those who are beset because of little chinks in their spiritual armor.

Been there? Done that? Me too!

One such incident took place in an African country some years ago. I happened to be at the missionary fellowship barbecue when this took place. It was the farewell party for a junior missionary about to go on furlough for a year. One official had a strong and differing opinion from him regarding how to go about ministering to university students. Animosity began to build.

The senior official spoke but not quite quietly enough. I heard it. He was speaking to another missionary and referring to the return of the junior missionary in a year's time. He had the authority. His feelings were quite strong as he said, "He will return to this field only over my dead body."

Unfortunately, that is exactly what happened. It was several years after the death of the senior missionary, who was really too young to die, that the junior missionary did return to the same field and did a good work.

If you read Ecclesiastes 5:2 and 1 Peter 2:1, you will realize how rash words can catch God's ear and even have consequence. You might want to look at Ephesians 4:31, Titus 3:2 and James 4:11.

> The tongue can be as dangerous as a spear... Many a person has impaled himself on his own words.

The tongue can be as dangerous as a spear. The heart decides on what comes out of it, bitter or sweet. And ears hear and register what is spoken. Once registered, there is no delete button. Many a person has impaled himself on his own words.

45 Why Christians Offend

I seldom go to theatres. Most films have no appeal to me. They have plots which are too fantastical to make sense, tell no story worth considering or are just a series of violent killings, car chases and eerie imaginings.

It was while watching what I thought was a rather innocuous film that a scene came on that showed a small country church with the congregation singing one of the old hymns that has been part of the Church's repertoire for a hundred years. Nothing wrong with that, except one thing.

Hollywood seems to take delight in depicting Christians as dowdily dressed people from the lower classes, typecasting them as simpletons and portraying them as mindless followers of an outdated and seeming superstitious belief system. The implications were that Church was a psychological crutch for dummies using it to escape from reality. Personally, I was offended.

Why is the simplicity of the gospel so offensive to judgmental individuals who feel so self-sufficient in their own intellect, positions of power, influence or wealth? Why is it that the gospel turns people off and gives them a sense of superiority? (Or is that conviction?)

By its very nature the gospel offends because it challenges the lifestyle and hidden sins of people who are not ready to acknowledge they are anything less than brilliantly perfect. And besides, they say, "I run my own life and no one else will tell me how to live!"

In Galatians 1:10-11, the apostle Paul wrote, *"For if I still pleased men, I would not be a bondservant of Christ."* In Galatians 5:11, we read that the cross is an offence to the unbeliever. Too bloody! Too demanding of a change in behaviour and belief!

So much so that in some countries it is illegal to follow the gospel—it is an offence, punishable by imprisonment, ostracization and even death.

I'm not implying that as Christians we make ourselves obnoxious but I've often reflected on the fact that seldom in North America is a Christian thrown in jail simply because of his faith.

Is that because we try to please the world too much rather than please God? I came away from that film feeling that perhaps my "light" is somewhat distorted by my own inadequacy and reluctance to be real and transparent about my faith in Jesus.

46 Visions

Although I've long forgotten her name, there was a woman in Verona, Ontario, who burst into tears when she saw me walk onto the platform of the church where I was to speak. It just happened that my uncle was the pastor of the church, and as I watched the woman sobbing, I asked my uncle just what might have caused it. Was she emotionally unstable? He too was puzzled. She was a sound and stable member of the church.

After the service I had no need to ask. She approached me at the church doors, and by now her face was glowing with what I can only describe as "the joy of the Lord." She told me her story.

One night several years earlier she had been awakened with a vision. She saw a missionary's face and a few houses surrounded by flames. The impression she had was of extreme danger. She had no idea who this missionary was since he was totally unknown to her. She said she got on her knees by her bed and prayed for several hours until the burden lifted. Then she added, "When I saw you walk onto the platform, I recognized your face as the one in the vision!"

Further confirmation was that, in the context of my sermon that morning, I had used an illustration of what had happened to my wife and me and the two other missionaries on that remote mission station. I was talking about God's power to protect us when we served Him in obedience and trusted our lives into His hands.

A tribal war had broken out around us and the fighting was intense. Many were killed. More than 240 huts were burned to the ground and at least one with a baby perishing in the flames. Our night watchman had been killed with a *rungu* (hand club with a large knot on the end) inside the boundaries of the mission station. Flames had approached through the dry grass toward the mission station but inexplicably stopped dead at the fence of the station, even though a breeze was blowing and the grass was just as dry as elsewhere. Special government forces came to protect us within a few hours, and we slept fully clothed with car keys in our pockets for several nights at their advice. Peace was finally restored.

We compared dates, and it was the very time and date of the incident. She in the night, and we in daylight on the other side of the world.

Here was a woman who had a relationship with God and who was sensitive to His voice and call. Here was a missionary who was grateful to God for such a woman of faith and obedience, and for the assurance of God's Word!

Look at Isaiah 43:2 and John 4:46-54. Has God changed? I think not.

47
Too Busy

"Go away; I'm too busy!" That's a statement I never ever heard from my father. Sometimes he would listen for a while then suggest that we could discuss whatever it was more fully when he wasn't under the momentary pressure. But he was never too busy to pay some quality attention.

Designing a book cover in Evangel - Kenya

I know what it's like to be too busy, and more often than not we bring it on ourselves. Some people, including me, are on the edge of being workaholics. If there is nothing to do we get edgy and look for something to do even if it is totally without meaningful purpose. Activity is essential to our peace of mind...we think.

There are times when I have to sit and think through a problem or situation. That is essential from time to time. But there are few times when I just sit and let my mind wander, ponder and wonder. Yet that too is essential occasionally. The mind needs rest as much as the body. The soul needs rest as much at the mind. And the spirit needs rest as much as the soul.

But all that takes time. Most of us claim we don't have enough time. That's true only because we don't pick our priorities with thoughtful care. Many things we do can be left totally undone and in the long run it will have no consequence whatever.

The only way to sort out our priorities is to stop being so busy and take time to spend in the presence of God and His Word. God said, *"Be still, and know that I am God"* (Psalm 46:10). Stop fidgeting, and get your thoughts and soul connected with the Divine for a while each day. Then your busyness will turn out to be less taxing.

Jesus said, *"Come aside...and rest a while"* (Mark 6:31) to His disciples. There is no sin in occasional inactivity except perhaps when you're trying to put off doing something you know *must* be done.

Rest is essential. Even employers have come to know that they get more productive output from their employees if there are break times in their work.

How much better for the Christian to take time out and spend it in relationship moments with God! Then your busyness will not be overwhelming.

48 Missionary Murderer

I was asked by my interpreter, Francis Mutumba, in Uganda, to go to the village of his uncle to pray there and ask God to lift a curse which had been on the village for many generations. It seemed everything went wrong for well over seven generations.

When I arrived, his uncle was sitting in the centre of the compound alone. Children had scattered behind houses and into the bush. They were afraid of white people. (If you don't behave, the white man will come and eat you—something like the old bogeyman stories North American kids were told for generations.)

Other elders appeared, and the women were called from their huts. They walked across the perfectly swept dirt compound on their knees and bowed their heads respectfully onto my

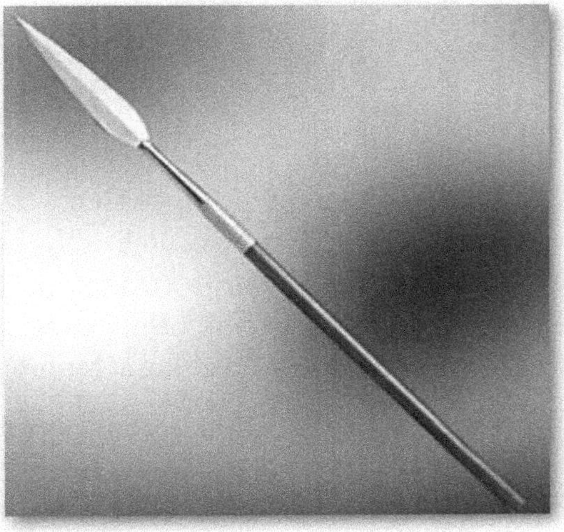

feet. I felt most uncomfortable. Eventually the whole story was told.

Ancestors from this village had been involved in the killing of the first four Church Missionary Society missionaries (led by Bishop Hannington) who had come to Uganda in 1885. One of the spears used to kill the missionaries had been hidden in the thatch roofs of succeeding village huts for all the generations since that time. When you read what Jesus said in Luke 11:49, that kind of thing can be expected. (Also read Malachi 2:2 and Matthew 5:21.) They felt that the curse on their village was associated with the spear.

Someone was sent to pull the thatch off the village chief's house and bring the spear to me. They asked me to take the spear away and, more importantly, to pray to my God that the curse would be lifted from their village. I told them the gospel story and explained Jesus and His power to the people gathered in the centre of the village. I did pray and Francis Mutumba translated the whole prayer.

God answered prayer. Months later I learned that the whole atmosphere of the village had changed and that many had become Christians. The curse was lifted. I have that spear to this day.

To the people of that Ugandan village that spear was the symbol of their rejection of God and His messengers. To me that same spear is a symbol of God's grace and forgiveness of a great injustice and sin.

And that's the point! God loves, forgives, delivers and saves anyone, no matter their history, hate, hopelessness or inheritance. God is love. He will deliver those who simply ask.

49 Bread

"Eat your crusts," my parents used to exhort me when I was a small child. I have no idea why I didn't like the crusts. Perhaps it was that they were too hard and hurt my gums. So I used to stash them away in one of my dresser drawers where they got even harder (and were found later by my mother—and mice).

When I was a little older I saved my pennies until I had the twelve cents necessary to buy a small fresh loaf of bread at the aromatic, drool-producing bakery I had to pass every day going to and from public school. That spoiled my appetite for supper more than once. But Oh! the taste and texture of warm fresh bread, including the crust!

Strange how we change as we get older! Now I love a fresh loaf of crusty bread or a narrow French loaf. The crust is part of the appeal.

Bread is mentioned in the Bible more than 250 times, two kinds of bread actually.

Just like nice crusty bread, the Bread of Life (Deuteronomy 8:3), God's Word, can hurt our spiritual gums by bringing us under conviction for sin. We try to set conviction aside and hide it from our conscious mind. Yet in Isaiah 55:2, we read, *"Why do you spend money for what is not bread, And your wages for what does not satisfy? Listen carefully to Me, and eat what is good, And let your soul delight itself in abundance."*

We so often waste our resources, whether time, money or skills, on things which just don't do us much good. We have a wealth of resources of many kinds but as we read in 1 Samuel 12:21—we invest in *"empty things which cannot profit or deliver."*

Bread is good for you. Don't disregard it until you're old, old enough to appreciate even the crusty "hard" parts, or until it is stolen by vermin.

50
9/11 to 2012

The world has changed dramatically since 9/11, when the two towering symbols of financial security were turned into rubble, and dust took precious lives into a sudden and terrifying eternity.

My niece's husband worked in that milieu and had moved three city blocks away from the twin towers just months before that horrid tragedy. She called me regularly throughout that terrible day asking me to pray for her husband. No word was heard, since the whole cell telephone system was overloaded. He finally arrived home at 11:00 p.m., filthy, tired and emotionally whipped. He lost many friends and associates that day.

All of North America responded in hundreds of ways to help on that disastrous day and for many weeks following.

Many human hearts were moved to take action in ways they had perhaps never before reacted. A terrible need was seen and extraordinary courage and sacrifice was made by many.

My niece's husband has always been a man of compassion for others. And he acts on it. His is not a faith which says, "I hope you make it through this disaster." He helps people through disaster. The list of his actions is recorded in heaven.

Throughout the world there continues to be great disasters and needs. Acts of terror are increasing. War, natural disaster and famine continue, yet in spite of exposure to these tragic realities many people just watch the next TV show.

In Proverbs 21:13, we read: "*Whoever shuts his ears to the cry of the poor Will also cry himself and not be heard.*"

When do you suppose we will realize that God operates on a completely different economy? He is neither intimidated nor bound by the fragile economies of humankind.

But *"My God shall supply all your need according to His riches in glory by Christ Jesus"* (Philippians 4:19).

Perhaps the world will yet change more drastically than any of us would dream!

51 Grace

Her name: Grace. I met her in Africa. She is married to Fred, who at one time was an uncouth, rough-living, reprobate and foul-tongued sailor. He had a remarkable conversion to Jesus Christ and though there were traces of his former rough edges, Grace had helped produce astonishing changes in Fred, in lifestyle, faith and even occupation. I have never met a more gracious woman than Grace. She lived her name.

When I say "Grace produced," I mean specifically the grace of God through Grace the woman.

Fred became fully involved in Christian missions and in the co-ordinating and writing of materials for African pastors in a series of books I had the privilege of publishing in Kenya called, "Theological Education by Extension" courses. Had you known Fred the sinner, you would be staggered by the change exhibited in Fred the saint. And it was all by the grace of God.

You'll find the expression "grace of God" often in the New Testament.

So what is grace, aside from being a very beautiful name? Simple put: grace is the undeserved, unearned favour of God even in the face of deplorable behaviour. That is why Paul writes in Ephesians 2:8-9 about this *"grace."* In fact in Acts 20:24, Paul refers to what he preached as *"the gospel of the grace of God."* We don't deserve it. It is ours as a gift.

The great tragedy in the Church today is that God's grace is all too often taken for granted and almost frittered away by the way we relate both to God and to people. Paul writes in 2 Corinthians 6:1: "*We then, as workers together with Him also plead with you not to receive the grace of God in vain.*" Read the rest of that chapter. True Christian ministry is exercised in grace, not according to what people deserve, but with that same unearned favour which does not discriminate no matter how hateful the circumstances. Being able to be gracious is clearly a gift of God.

It is grace which enables us to turn the other cheek, accept abuse, and remain steady in faith and in conduct. That's a big order . . . but it is an order!

It's one of those peculiarly "Christian things."

52 Who Owns the Offering?

The giving of offerings for the work of the Lord is a part of Christian responsibility. The Bible has a great deal to say about giving in tithes, offerings, alms to the poor and for special projects. Both the Old and New Testaments are rife with examples of godly giving.

Such giving is what will be rewarded by God. The rewards sometimes even appear in this earthly life. There is no doubt that it will be rewarded in eternity. We are laying up treasures in heaven for ourselves when we give to God.

Don't ask me just how God will reward us in heaven. I have very little notion of how that might be. Special gilt on the windows of your mansion seems unlikely. We need only take God's Word for it (Matthew 6:19-20). God's ways are His and His alone. He is Sovereign in all areas of life.

Yet there are some who, having given something to God, perhaps even in an emotional high, have regretted it and want to "reclaim" it.

I've seen it happen. A person gave money to a ministry then disagreed strongly with something that ministry did and asked for their donation to be returned to them. In Proverbs 20:25 we read *"It is a snare for a man to devote rashly something as holy, And afterward to reconsider his vows."*

All this raises a very basic question: "Who was that offering given to—the man, the ministry or to God?" Our responsibility as Christians is to give to God, and we will be held accountable for the giving. If a ministry misuses those funds, that ministry leadership will be called to account before God—either in this life or the next, or both.

There is a flaw in the character and understanding of any person who gives to God, then tries to get it back. Christian leadership should teach biblical truth about these matters. Yet there can also be a flaw in the character of the leadership in ministry. This must be the responsibility of other Christians to deal with in a biblical manner.

Read Galatians 6:1 for instruction for both situations, giver and receiver.

53 Attitude Is Everything

Some things I don't like. Painting is one of them. I find it frustrating. My hands get all sticky with paint. Little specks of paint spot my face when I paint with a roller. Paint runs onto my hands when I paint with a brush. I almost invariably lean against a wet area of paint, which ruins a shirt. It is difficult to repaint unless you let it dry so that you can sand away the imprint of the fabric. I think you get the message. I don't like painting.

My cousin Ken was moving into town to semi-retire. The house they had bought stunk with the smell of cigarette smoke. (*Another* thing I don't like: the stink of cigarettes.) It needed painting. So my son and a friend and I threw ourselves into the job. We laughed and enjoyed the application of a new aroma to the house. In the process, we found a little "grow-op" hidden under the stairs by the previous tenant. When we were done painting, there was a deep sense of satisfaction at a job well done—at least in our opinion.

We had gone into it with the right attitude, in spite of apprehensions, dislikes and the state of the house.

Attitude is everything. When Moses sent twelve spies into the Promised Land they all went in with at least a few preconceived notions. Ten spies came back with negative reports and democracy won the day. But who ever said democracy was *always* right? As a result Israelites by the thousands wandered in the wilderness for forty years. They had adopted the attitude of others.

Your attitude, your demeanour, your words and your actions can set the tone and be a model for those around you—for good or for bad. It seems most people are more ready to pick up on the bad than the good. The results can be immediate or reserved for the future.

In Numbers 14:36-38 we read that Joshua and Caleb were the only two of the twelve spies who survived the forty years in the wilderness. Not only did they survive, but Joshua led Israel in to the Promised Land with great victories, and Caleb was eighty-five years old when he conquered a mountain and laid personal claim to it!

It just doesn't pay to be negative. I prefer the "I can do it" attitude, though I still don't like painting!

54 Joy

An African Christmas is one of the most joyful experiences I have ever had. It is tiring. It lasts for most of the day. Singing, rejoicing, clapping of the hands to enthusiastic drumbeats and periodic preaching and teaching, and yes, a feast! It's all about Jesus and how He provided the bridge back to God. That's the kind of joy that never ends.

On the other hand, Christmas in North America is one of few happy times of year, especially for children. The look on their faces when they open each gift—pure happiness! Wonderful lights and decorations set the tone for this highlight of the Christian calendar. Throngs and bouquets, songs and banquets, games and gifts! Family, friends and fun! These are the happenings of Christmas. They pass.

That's the difference between joy and happiness. One sticks, the other slips away.

One of the ways to produce happiness for both the rich and the poor is for the rich to give to the poor. But all that will pass, both for the rich and for the poor. Things that happen are temporary. Joy lasts forever and has one source. Happiness depends on what "happens!"

In Psalm 43:4 we discover where to find true joy: *"Then I will go to the altar of God, to God my exceeding joy; and on the harp I will praise You, O God, my God."*

For the Christian, joy is something which is born in the heart and lasts through all of life. 1 Peter 1:8 says: *"whom having not seen you love. Though now you do not see Him, yet believing, you rejoice with joy inexpressible and full of glory."*

Gifts can be lost or stolen. Happiness flees.

The gift of God is the abiding presence of Jesus which cannot be suffocated no matter what the happenings or terrors around.

I've seen the stark reality of that truth in the middle of the horrors meted out to the Christians of Southern Sudan by godless gangsters attributing their motivation and methods to a god who is not a god at all.

Similar things are done in the business world in North America because some people just can't get enough to make them happy. What they really need is the joy of the Lord.

55 Difficult Duty

I saw the most dreadful duty I had ever seen being performed during the starvation days in the early 1980s in Ethiopia. It shocked me, made me cry, made me angry and changed my life forever. It caused my career to move in a new direction.

We had been involved in emergency feeding for about a year when I was in Ethiopia for a trip to monitor and report back to our television audience what was happening with the $3,000,000 dollars our viewers had donated and the $5,000,000 of aid from the Canadian government. My trip called for a helicopter lift into one of the feeding stations.

Inside the thorn fence surrounding the compound where only about sixty tonnes of corn was available, I was in conversation with the administrator of the feeding program. I looked up and saw a young medic at the gate looking at the hundreds, indeed thousands of people approaching the gate, one at a time. He was sending them in two different directions. I asked what was happening. I was shocked at the answer.

"He is choosing between those we can feed and those we cannot feed," was the answer. Many hundreds had already been turned away. Only a comparative few were being chosen to receive food. Why? Because they had to choose between keeping everyone alive for a few days longer or keeping a minority alive until the next shipment of food came, probably months away. There simply wasn't enough to go around to the many emergency feeding stations.

I was horrified. I had been feeling good about the amount of food we were getting into Ethiopia. Hundreds of thousands of tonnes! But it was not enough. I came from the fat end of the stick, and that young medic had to handle the lean end.

That night I rolled and tossed until dawn. I had come to a decision. If I was to be a leader I would do everything in my power to never let this happen again. I wasn't even sure I wanted to be a leader anymore, but I made a decision—a hard and significant decision. It has affected me, my family and even my friends.

Leadership has responsibilities. Often they are difficult and onerous.

Don't look for leadership just for the glory, because most often it's not very glorious.

56 Justice

I have, thus far, been into Sudan more than 45 times. I have seen injustice in its worst form. Slavery by the Islamist Arabs of the north has been carried out as a weapon of war against the black, predominantly Christian south of Sudan. There has been rape, the genocide of thousands and robbery by bands of militia descending with guns and flame on innocent villagers. While peace talks were in progress, bombs were still being dropped on schools, churches, hospitals, markets and wherever a crowd might gather. The injustice of it all is what drives me to do something about it.

Why? Because I am a Christian! And that's why you too should do something about it. Many years will pass before Sudan is stable even if the peace agreement does in fact hold.

Justice is one of the primary themes of the Bible. One hundred and twenty-nine times it either calls for it or points out where justice has been perverted. The first laws given to man by God were that we should not pervert justice (Deuteronomy16:19). In 1 Kings 3:11, we see how God gave a lot more than Solomon's request to discern justice when he asked God for that gift.

Justice does not grow out of pride or arrogance. It is a part of the humble life (Psalm 25:9). And we are instructed in Psalm 82:3 to *"defend the poor and fatherless; Do justice to the afflicted and needy."*

Because of the terror reigning in Sudan by the north against their own south, Proverbs 13:23 is a living fact. The south of Sudan has about one and a half million internally displaced persons still in 2012. All of this because of the north's lust for oil and the natural riches of the south (Proverbs 16:8).

We who live in North America are even ready to sacrifice to allow for justice in such situations. But what about justice in your own neighbourhood, your city and your nation? Have you ever raised your voice? In Proverbs 21:3, we read what God thinks of that: *"to do righteousness and justice Is more acceptable to the LORD than sacrifice."*

We don't have to be concerned about punishing those who do injustice (Proverbs 21:7). God will look after that. As Jesus said to the Pharisees in Matthew 23:23, the answer for us as Christians is not in the show we put on, but in the justice we show.

57 Kindness

A young man I had known was up against hard times. Had he not received the $400 I had given him he would have lost his house. Note, I said I had given it to him. When I give something to people I give it as a gift. It's an example my father set before me. "Give," he said, "not expecting to get it back again." Luke 6:30 says: *"Give to everyone who asks of you. And from him who takes away your goods do not ask them back."*

Forty-five years ago Mary and I had gone through the same situation. We were out of cash pastoring our first small church. We had no food to feed a group of visiting students from the Bible college. An Lutheran butcher offered to saw a frozen turkey in half and I was to pay when I could. We were able, with a few potatoes plus vegetables in dinted cans we bought from a local cannery, to feed them a virtual feast—not to mention the turkey sandwiches we enjoyed for a few days following.

We eventually paid him and bought the other half. A very kind butcher!

Those two verses in Luke 14:13-14 give us the biblical basis for such actions. *"And you will be blessed, because they cannot repay you."*

Peter wrote about this sort of thing in 2 Peter 1:5-7. Faith will grow on you, in you, and perhaps even through you, as you show kindness to others. Paul also tells us how we should act in many ways toward others. Colossians 3:12-13 says: *"Therefore, as the elect of God, holy and beloved, put on tender mercies, **kindness,** humility, meekness, longsuffering; bearing with one another, and forgiving one another, if anyone has a complaint against another; even as Christ forgave you, so you also must **do.**"*

That's how Christians are *supposed* to act. Rather than random acts of gossip, the demeaning of others and recounting another's weaknesses and highlighting their low points try looking for a way to be kind, denying the devil a foothold in your life.

Kindness brings more joy to the giver than to the one who receives.

58 Hypocrisy

It sounded so hollow.

The man, purportedly a refugee, had come by his riches through fraud in the freeing of slaves in Sudan. As a refugee living in a neighbouring country, he did not live in the squalor of the refugee camps as thousands of other did. He owned three houses in the capital, owned three large four-wheel drive vehicles and often partied with friends. All of this acquired through corruption.

At the final "Comprehensive Peace Agreement" for Sudan, he stood with great piety and spoke of the need for an exemplary, clean, transparent and corruption-free government in the south. Then he added, "God bless us in our future." At this writing, his wife has died of AIDS, and he is in hospital, dying. So much for a "clean" future!

To me, knowing the facts, it sounded so hollow.

I have often pondered the question, "Why doesn't God strike a person dead when they invoke His Name in the middle of their own unrighteousness?" Actually, I am glad He doesn't because I too would likely be dead.

Perhaps you've had the same experience as I have. A simple and seemingly harmless thing! Perhaps there was a sharp argument with a family member just before you entered church. Then, your frown turned suddenly into a smile for everyone, and a veneer of pious spirituality was pasted in place for the duration of the service. You came away from church still empty and hollow because of the hypocrisy of the moment. Been there, done that?

Rather than strike us dead, God has offered a gate, the answer—if we just adjust our attitude and ask, as in Psalm 118:19-20, *"Open to me the gates of righteousness; I will go through them, And I will praise the LORD. This is the gate of the LORD, Through which the righteous shall enter."*

Live righteously and praise God with confidence. Proverbs 18:10 says: *"The name of the LORD is a strong tower; The righteous run to it and are safe."*

59 Is Life All About Me?

Some lessons you *almost* learn when you are very young. It's not until many years later that you may be faced with a situation which demands, not just the recall of the "almost learned" lesson, but also the application of it.

My father, with a reputation for a certain degree of sternness and an unflinching commitment to integrity, tried to tell me. But too often the ears of a twelve-year-old are more easily attuned to the sound of an exciting baseball game going on at the empty corner lot. The voice of a patient father trying to give his offspring a clue to human relationships which could and would soon demand attention had much less appeal.

So when Dad was outlining a very simple truth to me it slipped out the other ear, all but one phrase which I *did* remember. Dad said, "Cal, you must realise that the world does not revolve around you." That phrase stuck.

Only rarely do children really absorb the simply profound. I certainly didn't, at least at that moment. My world was revolving around me and making me almost dizzy with the wonderful prospect of being pleased with what *I* wanted to do.

"There's nothing wrong with a good baseball game," I argued (to myself, quietly in my own mind). And I was right of course. A twelve-year-old is always right. Just ask him!

It was just my timing and attitude which were wrong. I learned of course. I realized my fault when my father's hand "revolved" near the seat of my pants. Much later, I also got the full impact on this subject from God when I read Proverbs 21:2; *"Every way of a man is right in his own eyes, But the LORD weighs the hearts."*

60 We'll Be Rich!

There are memories which ignite regret.

A preacher from North America was invited to preach in a church in the middle of the Mathari Valley, a slum settlement found almost in the centre of Nairobi, Kenya. He preached a "prosperity doctrine" which was extremely attractive to the people living in cardboard and tin shacks with open sewers and surrounded by filth and poverty. The crowds grew until the little shack church was crowded beyond capacity. The preacher returned to North America under the impression that hundreds had come to know Jesus Christ and that his trip was a great success.

What he left behind was another matter entirely. People thought, *"We'll all be rich!"* When they began to put into practice the principles and formulae he had taught them, they found that it didn't quite work that way. God did not miraculously pour down wealth on them. They remained mired in their poverty. The church dwindled. Even those whom the Kenyan pastor had gathered and had begun to be grounded in God's word finally dissipated. The church died; gone without a trace.

Why? Because half-truths are as deceptive and dangerous as outright lies!

The greatest wealth anyone can have is a living relationship with God through Christ and with His Church. Even though many Scriptures show that God supplies our needs, answers our prayers and cares for His own, there are conditions. God puts a few "ifs" on many of His promises.

Life does not consist of the things we possess for all too often those "things" possess ***us***. God is not interested in pouring wealth out on us so that we can fulfil our own carnal desires. He blesses us with material blessings to bless others through the gospel of Jesus Christ.

The apostle Paul was a tent-maker and said he knew how to abound and how to be abased. He *worked* with his hands to support himself while he laboured for the Lord. Proverbs 6:10-11 has something to say about this. Poverty comes to those who disdain correction and to those who do not share and to those who are lazy.

It's not wrong to be wealthy. It's not a sin to be poor.

But it ***is*** a sin to teach half-truths which leave people with false hopes. When the "whole counsel" of God is preached, there is balance in the Church and in individual Christians' lives. God will supply all our *need*s and even many of our desires.

The greatest wealth anyone can have is a living relationship with God through Christ and with His Church.

In North America we are too often taken up with the comforts of this life than we are with the glorious truth that one day we will be "taken up." It may sound trite, but you *can't* take it with you!

61 What Does God Heal?

Memory is a tricky thing.

I recall praying for a little boy in Uganda who apparently suffered some devastating disease, possibly polio, which left him so crippled he was taken about in a handmade wooden wheelbarrow. Even the wheel was wooden. He sat in the wheelbarrow with his feet folded under him, legs like sticks with clubs at both ends, calloused edges on the sides of his feet, but with an upper body which seemed in somewhat better condition, except his arms.

When I prayed for him nothing happened, immediately. Three days later I was called by the pastor to come and see the boy who was running around with fully fleshed-out legs, playing football with others boys his age. I hesitated in believing it was the same boy, until the pastor called him and showed me the calluses still on the outside edges of his feet and his soles, which had baby tender skin, blistered from walking and running. He was as happy a boy as I had seen.

I don't remember the many, many people I have prayed for who were *not* healed. Memory can be selective. I remember the wondrous miracles but not those who were disappointed, both in God and perhaps in me.

But all this has led me to some important conclusions. God ***does*** still heal people. I've seen it too often to be able to rationalise and explain it away as some other phenomenon. I've also come to understand that God does not heal people *of* old age. He heals people *in* their old age, but not of their old age.

I have also concluded that God is Sovereign in everything! He has a plan which includes all people, everywhere, and He knows how best to work out His plan.

Long ago I also became aware of the fact that I am not the centre of the universe. God is!

My responsibility is to worship God, and ask God for His grace and mercy on myself and others. I have been taught from God's Word to anoint with oil and lay hands on the sick for healing. God then decides just what kind of answer fits into His plan, and acts accordingly.

He is God!

62 Blasphemy

Blasphemy has been in the news in this past year or so. There have been accusations of blasphemy against a man, with threats to another man's life. Some lives have been threatened because they talked negatively about Mohammed. There have been charges of blasphemy levelled against the producers of a film depicting Jesus Christ in a most unflattering and erroneous scenario. Boycotts and threats of retribution have been levelled against the blasphemers. But read 1 Samuel 2:25.

What is blasphemy?

The first mention of it is found in the law which God gave to the Israelites (Leviticus 24:16). Blasphemy is only truly blasphemy when it is levelled against God Himself. Chatter against any person is just libel or slander.

Humankind is not divine, no matter the prophetic claims, reputation or gifts. If you read Hebrews 10:28-29 you'll find that blasphemy is not an insignificant thing! It has consequences of eternal proportions.

Those who blaspheme the Lord are literally taking their lives in their hands and must realize that they have challenged God Himself. But there is hope, even for one who blasphemes against the Lord Jesus Christ. Read Luke 12:10: *"And anyone who speaks a word against the Son of Man, it will be forgiven him; but to him who blasphemes against the Holy Spirit, it will not be forgiven."* There seems to be a fine line not to be crossed.

Forgiveness is available for those who truly repent, except in those extremely rare cases where a person deliberately and knowingly blasphemes the Holy Spirit of God.

Godless people should be very thoughtful before they decide to mock God! It's not cold enough to walk on the thin ice where they are going.

And Christians, too, should be very careful in respect to the kind of jokes they share when using the name of the Lord. God is God, Holy and Sovereign.

Because we live in a society which has become altogether too liberated and lawless does not lessen our need to understand the awe and holiness of the Lord.

63 Serious Cheats

When we lived in Kenya as missionaries we would occasionally get together with other missionary families for games, such as Rook, Monopoly or Scrabble. Some of us would play chess. Some of us would cheat. In our case, it was almost invariably preplanned as a lark and discovered quite early in the game. The cheaters would humbly repent and we'd all have a laugh. Then we'd start over again playing the game honestly.

It was at that stage when Mary would serve her Chelsea buns. Sometimes the games got a bit sticky with the wonderful globs of cinnamon on the buns. Pieces of the Scrabble game often had to be washed.

Nobody likes a serious cheater at table games such as Monopoly or in a written exam. The result can be harsh and very well remembered. Things can get sticky without the involvement of sticky buns. A cleanup is essential.

We have read of cheaters who take advantage of their positions as heads of corporations. One is currently serving years in prison for the largest corporate fraud in American history. He cheated thousands of people out of their life savings. Their retirement is now a painful and angry existence. No one likes that particular cheater.

It's in that connection that it would be a good idea to read Colossians 2:18-23. It starts off: *"Let no one cheat you of your reward, taking delight in false humility."* It has deeper implications—implications which can rob you of your liberty in Jesus Christ. This kind of cheating can lead you into religious rules and extreme legalism that tie you in knots and lead you away from the freedom found only in Christ.

Earlier in the same chapter, verse 8, we read the foundation on which this kind of cheating takes place. It is through *"philosophy and empty deceit, according to the tradition of men, according to the basic principles of the world, and not according to Christ."*

Unfortunately, there are a few serious cheats who become "religious leaders." They use religion as their vehicle and the religious as their target. We've seen it happen in the perversion of Islam by Islamist Fundamentalists. But don't think it only happens in Islam. Paul warns us here in these Scriptures that it can happen within the Christian faith.

Don't be deceived by charismatic personalities. Their characters may be very sticky. Some may be serious cheats! Avoid them. Wash your hands of them!

"Let no one cheat you of your reward, taking delight in false humility."

Colossians 2:18-23

64 Saying the Right Thing

I cannot forget a time in Africa when I was trying to impress an African brother in Christ that it was his Christian duty to pay his debts. He happened to owe a good sum of money for a high quality Bible he had bought from the publishing house I was managing.

He did not hear what I said very clearly and interpreted it as a racist slur. I *had* spoken harshly and with some emphasis but there was no personal or racist intent in what I said. It made no difference, and what he thought I had said spread like wildfire among some of the Africans who lived near or on the mission station. It took a long while before that boiling kettle simmered down. What I had said was true but the way I said it was absolutely wrong. Rather than something being lost in the translation, it was "found." I could not help but think of James 3:6: *"the tongue is a fire, a world of iniquity. The tongue is so set among our members that it defiles the whole body, and sets on fire the course of nature; and it is set on fire by hell."*

Attitude can be just as bad as, or worse than, the words we speak.

Saying the right thing does not always come easily. Yet the things which come out of our mouth, though right and accurate, can be either harmful or destructive. Our words can encourage or discourage, build or destroy, burn or dampen. Shading the truth by shying away from speaking plainly or trying to please the ears of other by being politically correct produces only confusion.

Sometimes the truth can do any or all of those things, simply because it is the truth, inflection, tone, timing and loudness aside. Truth itself often hurts no matter how kindly it is delivered.

Balaam, a prophet of God, was under pressure to prophecy according to the wishes of Balak, king of Moab. They'd already gone through two prophecies which didn't go down well with Balak and the princes of Moab. So Balak tried to strike a deal. In Numbers 24:13, Balaam finally said what had to be said in the face of king and princes. *"If Balak were to give me his house full of silver and gold, I could not go beyond the word of the LORD, to do good or bad of my own will. What the LORD says, that I must speak."*

It often puts you at odds with society and is interpreted as politically incorrect, but the truth, God's truth, must prevail come hell or high water, silver or gold. We cannot afford to sell our tongues or even rent them out. The stakes are too high.

65 My Prize Python

Snakes in Africa come in various sizes, colours and degrees of danger. Some are in the ocean, most others are on land. The great majority you never see. It's the minority which speed up the heart and give an adrenaline rush. I am not immune to reacting to snakes. I don't much like them.

It was not the first python I had seen in Africa but it was the first one I had seen in the act of crushing its prey before it would swallow it slowly. Its victim was the smallest gazelle in Africa, called a dik-dik, with a body about the size of a rabbit. The ten foot long python had crawled up a bush, wrapped around the dik-dik and set its head about eye level with me. He was too busy to pay any attention to me. I rushed and got a shotgun out of our tent, where we had camped while hunting for game for our larder.

Dik-dik

One blast from my shotgun brought an end to the snake. Since the skin was

undamaged I knew I had a prize python skin to have tanned. The dik-dik was dead. Just as the python was approaching victory it lost - badly.

I skinned it and took the skin in to a tanner in Nairobi. I was going back to get it a few weeks later. I was going to have a conversation piece to outclass many others. When I did go back weeks later to get it I was told that it had been stolen. Just as I thought I had a great prize it was snatched from me. I knew because of its quality it had "taken flight" and I would never see it again.

Two losers: the python and me. Of course I was upset!

Life is often very much like that. Just when all your planning, working and hoping seem to be coming to success, something goes haywire. Strangely, at other times, with no plans and little effort you find yourself blessed with a wonderful prize not of your own making.

The Lord gives and the Lord takes away (Job 1:21)! We came in to this world naked, and that's the way we leave. In between the two events, birth and death, it is amazing how much we collect with some vague notion we can somehow crowd it all into our coffin for eternity. That's the mindset of the pagan world.

Christians believe what Jesus said in Luke 12:15; *"Take heed, and beware of covetousness, for one's life does not consist in the abundance of the things he possesses."* And if anyone should know, it would be Jesus. He inhabits both time and eternity.

Just when all your planning, working and hoping seem to be coming to success, something goes haywire...

Theology

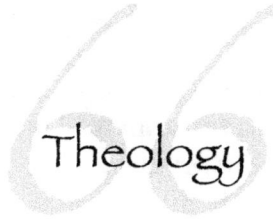

Theology is the study of God.

Theologians bring us definitions, clarifications, insights and theories into the person and nature of God. They are not always based on the Bible alone, but should be. Theologians serve a very useful purpose and are essential to maintaining our understanding of God within the confines of divinely revealed Scripture. Theologians protect us against heresies, spiritual aberrations and foolish interpretations of the Bible. The study of Scripture is absolutely essential to every Christian. Paul the Apostle tells us to study the Scriptures and rightly interpret them (2 Timothy 2:15).

Theological truth must remain true to Scripture from beginning to end. Every theological truth must be in total concert with the all of the Bible, both content and context.

Through a lack of attention to the details of biblical revelation many preachers have made havoc of the lives of their followers by presenting half-baked ideas which do not resonate with the whole of Scripture. Thus cults, heresies and strange doctrines come and go like the hula hoop. Jesus said, *"My words shall not pass away"* (Matthew 24:35 KJV). Psalm 119:89 states, *"forever, O LORD, Your word is settled in heaven."* Solid biblical teaching remains the only anchor for our faith and for our practical everyday living as Christians.

But theology remains pointless unless it brings us into a better understanding of God and into a closer relationship with Him.

Theology is not merely a matter of memory of a catechism, statements of faith or creeds. There exists the distinct possibility that we can reduce (and I do mean "reduce") our understanding of God the Almighty to a few true, clear and refined sentences and paragraphs which define God well. But even if our intellectual understanding of God is at the highest level yet we do not draw near to Him personally through Jesus Christ, it is just so many words on a paper or in a mind.

The greatest impact of theology blossoms when the truth "about" God becomes a personal walk and acquaintance "with" Him. Theology is not an end in itself. To know God personally and progressively and more intimately is the grand goal of true theology.

Jesus warned His followers to listen to the truth of the theologians of His days among men, but He clearly told them not to live like them (Matthew 23:1-12). They had truth but did not practice it.

Have you done your practicing today?

67 The Hyena

When we lived for seventeen years in Africa, financial support was often inadequate. We simply had to make do with what we had. Wildlife abounded, and for $15 a hunting license was available. I was also able to buy a rifle. Part of our larder was meat from hunting in the Loita Plains among the Maasai people. We usually went to a place called Moji Moto (hot water). A natural hot mineral water spring gurgled from under a rock, providing a year-round green area in an otherwise desolate plain.

I took my son John with us one time. He was just over three years of age. After a day's hunt, we would hang our meat high in nearby trees to cool at night and high enough that the all-too-common hyena could not get at it. At the altitude of the Loita Plains it could get cold enough that occasionally a skim of ice would be on our water containers by morning.

After our evening meal of wild guinea fowl and canned vegetables, we sat around the campfire at night and traded exaggerations until it was time to crawl into our tents.

Out of the corner of my eye I saw the glint of eyes in the bush reflecting the firelight. I looked more closely and discerned a hyena. Not uncommon. But in this case the hyena was stealthily getting ready to pounce on my son on the opposite side of the fire from me. I leapt to my feet, over the fire, grabbed John and lifted him quickly into the entrance to our tent. I scared him, since he had no idea he was about to be attacked. I told neither John nor my wife Mary about that until some years later.

But I'm convinced I saved my son's life that night. Hyenas have been known to snatch small children. They exert a pressure of about 700 pounds per square inch with their jaws. I didn't want that fate for my well-loved, adopted son.

I wonder how many times God saves us from unknown dangers and even frightens us sometimes in the process?

68 Longsuffering

Bob, a friend of mine in Nairobi, was caught in a very bad traffic jam in a roundabout. He could move no more than a few inches forward or backward. The driver of a truck on his left yelled at him to get out of the way or, he said, he'd ram into him. He had become impatient, though he was by far not the only one who was losing patience with the total gridlock. Bob decided he was just letting go of steam because it was apparent that he could not move. No one could move.

Suddenly the engine of the truck roared and the truck driver turned its front wheels and drove right into the side of Bob's car.

What would you have done? There was little Bob could do. Now his door was crushed and he couldn't even get out of his car. Bob was a Christian. He reacted as a Christian should. He just sat there. It's called longsuffering. Bob did get the truck driver's license number for insurance purposes. But that was little use in Kenya in those days. Rather than pay for your car's repair, they gave you five years of free insurance. What's that all about? Just another call for more longsuffering!

Paul points out in Galatians 5:22 that one of the fruits of the Spirit is longsuffering. In our high speed society, impatience and anger too often betray the Spirit within us. If we are partakers of the divine nature should we not yield to the still small voice within us rather than to the loud and raucous voices around us? Why should we imitate the world, which is bound for perdition? Already too much of the world has leached into Christ's church.

Impatience and anger too often betray the Spirit within us. Why should we imitate the world, which is bound for perdition? Already too much of the world has leached into Christ's church.

Paul reinforces the need for longsuffering to young Timothy (2 Timothy 3:10), the Colossians (3:12) and the Ephesians (4:2). It might be well to give heed to these verses and their context for the good of our own spirits and with a higher regard for the Spirit who dwells within us.

It is hard to do, but do it we must. We do represent the gentle Spirit of God after all!

69 Love

I was in grade one when I first "fell in love." The girl who caught my eye had jet black hair and was cute. Her name was Veronica. I "fell in love" a half-dozen times after that. It took a while before I discovered that real love has nothing to do with merely sentimental feelings. I grew up and was able to discern the difference between liking, romancing, preferring, caring, lusting and all the various forms of what are considered love by our modern society. I chose who to court based on *some* of those feelings *and* on a much more rational level as well. I *chose* the love of my life, and she was blonde; still is blonde occasionally. Love is a much more full-blown reality than some assume.

Hollywood has slowly narrowed love down to mere lust as illustrated by many serial marriages. That of course has skewed much of the movie-watching world. Marriages last now only as long as people *feel* like staying married. Commitment is rare and is often conditional. Pre-nuptials! A rash of adultery is the natural result of an unnatural concept of love.

True love lasts through thick and thin. True love does include many of the elements described above which are feeling-oriented. But time and circumstances put huge dints into human feelings. Only true love can survive the bumps and thunder.

Love, to be genuine, is a deliberate long-term commitment. It is selfless and self-sacrificing. It is a 100 percent resolution and rigidity of purpose. It is patterned after the love of God. It is unchanging, unconditional and needs no prenuptial agreement. God loves with a steadfast dedication which is irreversibly fixed. That kind of love costs. At times it really hurts to love that way. John 3:16 emphasises this.

Mary and I have been married now for well over 50 years. There have been times when we didn't like each other but our commitment to each other was not only legal but also spiritual and final. That overcame the way we "felt" about each other's weaknesses and shortcomings. I can't imagine life without Mary.

The Apostle Paul, in 1 Corinthians 13:1-8, describes love, ending with *"love never fails."* Roman 13:8 and Galatians 5:14 are worth reading, too. It affects your relationships with everyone.

I can't imagine life without knowing the love of God personally.

By the way, Mary's hair is light brown with blonde and grey streaks as I write this. Kinda pretty!

70 Flattery

O'Flattery is not an Irish surname.

Everyone likes a compliment. I appreciate compliments. To speak well of people is by far a better attitude than pointing out someone's every weakness and fault.

On the other hand, we should be a little cautious about being too absorbent to the sounds of praise and fame which people try to put on us. Who knows what they really want? And when it becomes an overwhelming flood of flattery we need to be especially cautious. Jesus said as much in Luke 6:26; *"Woe to you when all men speak well of you."*

Your very reaction to flattery may set off a string of gossip based on how you take it.

Two terrible things can come out of too much flattery. Our ego can be filled with helium to the point of implosion when the flattery diminishes. We ought not to think more highly of ourselves than is appropriate. It is quite appropriate to have a good measure of self-confidence. It is better that others have confidence in you than for you to have too much in yourself.

The second attitude produced by flattery can be one of judgment: judgment of others as to how they measure up to you and what others purport you to be. That leads to assigning your negative reflections on others, followed by the use of your lips. It can turn into the acid of gossip.

I have never met a "right-thinking" gossip. Their whole attitude is skewed by a mind that seems eternally set on forming uninformed opinions of others. Thoughts, actions and attitudes are based on scattered bits and pieces of information and disinformation they have received from others. Fact and fancy are churned into a volatile mix.

There are quite a few references to the misuse of the tongue, but a summary is found in Proverbs 20:19: *"He who goes about as a talebearer reveals secrets; Therefore do not associate with one who flatters with his lips."*

There is a dangerous bond between gossip and flattery. O'Flattery is rarely legitimate. It is born of a bad marriage.

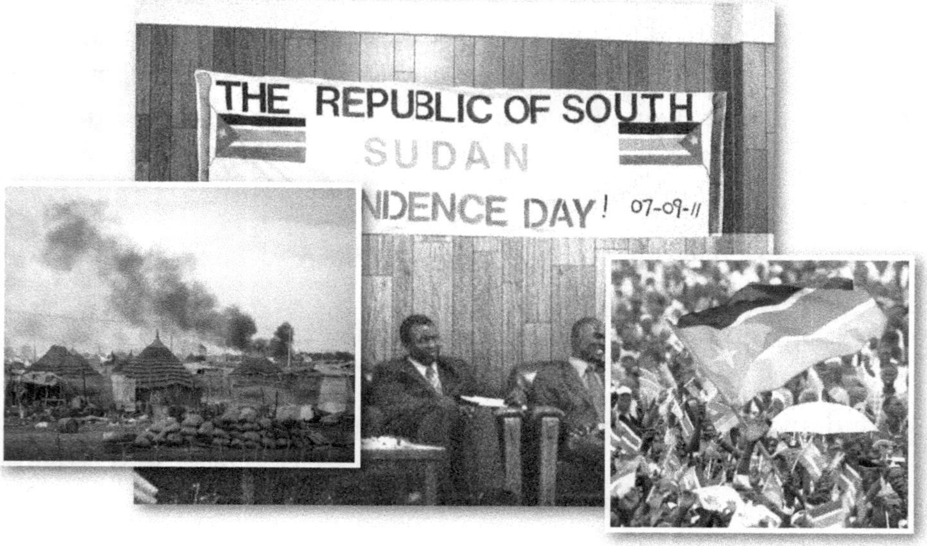

71 Where Is God?

I was reminded in 2011 of an incident that had happened at least 10 years previously. It was the Chairman of the Education Committee, The Honourable James Duku Yanka, in the government of the newest democracy on earth, the Republic of South Sudan. Yanka referred in a public speech to a time I spent overnight in a ruined guest house while bombs were landing nearby. "He risked his life with us."

I had forgotten that he was actually there during that experience, since he was simply another Southerner among many trying to survive a war already more than 40 years in progress. His reminder brought back the memories in detail. The remains of the house were perched on the side of a rocky hill in the town of Kajo Keji where 70,000 people once lived and where less than 7,000 were still hiding in nearby forests scrambling for enough food to support life.

We were all tired. We were all hungry. Bombs had been falling from the sky from high-flying Antonov bombers from the northern regime in Khartoum. We might or might not be alive through the night and into the next day. I was with Christians, but nearby there were traitorous southerners on the payroll of the north.

A bit farther up the rock strewn road from this precipitous shelter with less than half its roof was the *totally* demolished town administrative centre. No roof and no walls to speak of.

Few white men had come anywhere near here to stay overnight in those days. They seemed to be surprised by my lack of fear. And quite literally I had no fear. "Lightning never strikes the same place twice," right? A heavy tropical downpour was pounding on what little was left of the tin roof.

I wanted to sleep and asked them where I should lay my sleeping bag. They gave me a place mostly free from direct rain. As a few bombs and several mortars exploded nearby I went to sleep.

The morning broke clear and sunny. I asked them, "When all this fighting is over, what are you going to do? How will you treat the enemies among you?"

"We shall forgive them!" At that point, I knew God was there, in them and close to me.

In the New Testament there was is a verse found in Matthew 28:18-20. Read it! I can't say I "felt" the presence of God in that situation, but there is no doubt in my mind that He was there. Doesn't God say in Exodus 33:14, *"My Presence will go with you, and I will give you rest"?*

Just because you don't *feel* God's presence doesn't mean He is not right there with you in whatever your circumstance. God is with you!

72

Money Buys What?

Money can buy almost anything. In the case of high profile criminals it seems even to be able to buy innocence. Cars, houses, toys, food, travel and even friends, or as I have seen, slaves: all available with money.

In Sudan, I was involved in the process of buying about 1,700 slaves, in order to set them free. It was an odd and highly strenuous mental exercise, since the buying of human beings is totally against my nature and natural instincts. We were freeing them from terrible bondage and abuse and delivering them back to family and clan. That eased the mind to a degree, but only a little.

Justice (or perhaps I should say, injustice) can be bought with money. Just because money seems to be the mainstay of modern life, we think it can do anything—if placed in the right hands.

Whatever happened to bartering? There seems to be a resurgence of the bartering system these days. "I'll trade you this for that." No money passes hands. That probably leaves the "tax man" with a dilemma. Isn't that just too bad....

While sifting through some of my father's papers after his death, I found a certificate of stock in a mining venture—hundreds of shares, bought for a few dollars back in the thirties. When I traced it back, thinking I'd found the mother lode, I found a defunct and abandoned mining operation. Money is a very volatile commodity. After World War II, the German mark became almost worthless. The stock market crash in the thirties led many to suicide. Confidence in coin can cause catastrophe. The year 2008 began another diminishing of money in devalued investments.

Money is a transient thing. Recent years have seen money and investments disappear like a fresh water river into the saltiness of the ocean.

Although many people make the acquisition of money their main aim in life, there are a few things, actually the main things of life, which money cannot buy. God's economy works on an entirely different basis. Here's a short list:

Happiness

Relationships

Peace of mind and soul

Spiritual power or blessing

Love

Read Isaiah 55:2, Luke 12:15 and Acts 8:20. The things that really count are beyond the reach of the purse or pocketbook.

73 Mistake Making

Some years ago I made a major mistake in Kenya as general manager of Evangel Publishing House. When I tried to move the location from up-country into the Nairobi area, I ran into a multitude of problems. What I failed to understand was that God had a time set. I jumped ahead of God and caused endless tensions.

We all make mistakes. And yes, we all commit sin from time to time, large or small. None of us is perfect, though both you and I have probably met people who assumed they are. They are always right, never at fault and are quite willing to let you know. That's their *first* mistake.

I've made many mistakes. I'd have to write a book to list them all. On the other hand, I, like you, probably have a tendency to forget most of them. There are some that stand out, can't be forgotten and affect us the rest of our lives. We're forgiven when we ask God and the people involved, yet they remain in memory.

One of the remarkable things about the Bible is its blunt and unapologetic honesty about the mistakes, blunders and follies of some of the greatest biblical leaders.

Moses, for instance, was raised in privileged circumstances, but as an Israelite among Egyptians. When he saw an injustice against an Israelite at one point, he killed the Egyptian perpetrator and thought he'd done right (Acts 7:24). At this point in his life Moses knew that God had chosen him for the task of delivering the Israelites from Egyptian bondage. He might as well start now!

Later, when he stepped in during a dispute among his own Israelite brethren, they reviled him and asked him if he would do to them what he had done to the Egyptian. In Acts 7:25 we read of Moses' supposition; *"For he supposed that his brethren would have understood that God would deliver them by his hand, but they did not understand."*

The fact was that God *would* deliver them by Moses' hand. But in God's timing, not when Moses assumed. We too must learn that if we jump in with both feet before God's time comes, people around us will not understand, even our best friends.

When walking with God, serving God and representing God we need to be sensitive not only to the task He has called us to do but also to the time God wants us to act.

Moses did not understand that God does His own work. I didn't understand that either those years ago. God does the work; we are merely the catalysts. If we stand firm in faith, we can also stand and watch the wonders God will do.

74

Cut From the Same Cloth

Christmas in Africa was always a fascinating experience. The whole day was spent in great celebration. As many as twenty churches in one area would come together for fellowship, singing, multiple sermons (some very long), feasting and rejoicing because of the birth of Jesus Christ. It started when people got there. It was announced for 10:00 a.m., usually started around noon and went on until sunset.

African Methodist choir

It was a very colourful affair! REALLY colourful! Every church would have its choir, which would sing two songs, one designated to be repeated by all choirs and another song of their own choice. The colour came in with the women's dresses.

The women in each church choir would buy a complete bolt of cloth. Every dress was made of the same cloth in the same design. Multi-coloured and loud patterns were used. Others were one solid colour, but always bright. One choir I'll never forget was in brilliant, vibrating and reflective chartreuse, a light, loud green which almost forced your eyes closed in the brilliant African sun.

Some things you never forget. About people!

One characteristic, perhaps not seen enough in Christians, always seemed to be noted in the minds of observers. Too often the lack of this characteristic is used as an excuse for someone to simply write off the Christian faith as inconsistent with what it teaches.

That characteristic is humility. Pride, arrogance, pomposity, superiority and haughtiness are not the basic building materials of Christian character. Humility is!

We are told in 1 Peter 5:5 that humility is a part of our submission to God. *"Likewise you younger people, submit yourselves to your elders. Yes, all of you be submissive to one another, and be clothed with humility, for 'God resists the proud, But gives grace to the humble.'"*

If our being clothed in humility is genuine and consistent, it will be remembered by anyone who sees. It is as memorable as a startlingly noticeable piece of clothing. And it is never competitive.

Pride, arrogance, pomposity, superiority and haughtiness are not the basic building materials of Christian character.

Humility is!

...And it is never competitive.

75 Armed With Humility

President Chiluba of Zambia was a Christian and had been in office about a year and a half at the time I was in Zambia with my son John to interview him for release on *100 Huntley Street,* a daily national Christian TV program in Canada. Both John and I were formally dressed for the occasion.

President Chiluba

The presidential palace was beautiful, surrounded by large flowering trees and lawns with proud peacocks wandering outside the open windows of the large state room in which I was doing the interview. We had to re-start when the peacocks sounded out their loud, proud calls. When the interview was over, President Chiluba and I sat together as John took some B-roll to insert into the tape when it was to be edited.

As John squatted down behind the camera to get some special shots the room echoed with the sound of the seat of John's pants tearing wide open. From that moment on he faced the president. Even as we left he backed out the door. President Chiluba must have thought him the most respectful and humble young man ever! More likely humbled!

Humility is not normally a natural trait. But when clothed with humility there are distinct advantages. It's worth seeking. In Zephaniah 2:3 we are told to *"seek righteousness, seek humility. It may be that you will be hidden In the day of the LORD's anger."*

Why would the Lord be angry? Solomon tells us in Proverbs 16:5 that a proud heart is an abomination to the Lord. Punishment is mentioned in the same verse. Solomon goes on to write in Proverbs 28:25 that people with proud hearts stir up strife and have no respect for God. And James writes in 4:6 that *"God resists the proud, But gives grace to the humble."*

Peter writes to us in 1 Peter 5:6: *"Therefore humble yourselves under the mighty hand of God, that He may exalt you in due time."*

It seems to me that being genuinely humble in a godly manner does not mean being subjugated and sensitively thin-skinned. What is really means is that you're subjected to God and have the skin of a rhino. Praise doesn't penetrate enough to give a swelled head.

76 The Great Put-On

When my grandchildren were small they were probably like many others. They played games. Tori would be "the mother" and Josh would be "the father." They put on what they saw as the attitudes of their own parents.

The "mother" will cuddle the dolls, feed them with bottles, change their diapers and generally do all the things a good mother would do. On the other hand, my grandson, much like any father, would be distracted by something much more interesting than playing dolls. As the "father," he had *more important* things to do. He'd fiddle with his bicycle, put a puzzle together or do some other "job." This was when they were young. They copied their parents and their obvious traits and actions.

When they were a little older they learned to put on other things. They found that they could manipulate their parents by putting on an act of pouting, sorrow and even depression. If it worked, they'd continue that "put on" until it literally became a habit and a way with them. It became a real part of them—until the parents finally twigged to what was happening. Then the parents put on a stern attitude of discipline mixed with love and offered alternatives. Slowly the child would "put off' those wrong approaches.

As parents we all went through this process, and surely received the unwelcome advice and observations of friends, such as childless couples and a few others—a bit of which was probably good objective observation.

Just like children, we as adults have learned to "put on" certain facades for the benefit of our observers and associates. Often underneath is something else. When we are constantly in the presence of others we keep putting on a front. That front can eventually become our character. It works from the outside in. Slowly but inevitably, we see the benefits of having certain attitudes and actions. We find that it improves relationships and gives us our own sense of satisfaction and peace. This works with Christians, too!

Do you suppose this is what Paul was thinking when he wrote in Colossians 3:12? *"Therefore, as the elect of God, holy and beloved,* ***put on*** *tender mercies, kindness, humility, meekness,* ***longsuffering****"* (emphasis added).

If you keep putting those things on long enough they will become a very part of your life's fibre, your character. They will not be a facade, but a reality.

And here we thought that God did those things to us, when in fact God tells us to take the initiative in these character-building attitudes.

Mother's 95th birthday - Many family absent

17 Mercy

I was sitting in a locked room at the airport in Ivory Coast accused of trying to enter the country illegally. That was simply not true. But the unbelieving immigration officers decided to confiscate my passport, lock me up and . . . I had no idea what they had in mind! So here I was, thousands of miles from home, with only my briefcase and a single chair in the room.

I had been advised by my travel agent in Nairobi that I did not need a visa to get into Ivory Coast, since it was a French speaking country, and one of Canada's official languages was French. I took his word for it. So I sat, unable to speak French, unable to explain myself, but able to read. I took out my little travelling New Testament and began to read. Who knew how long I would be here? Better to occupy my mind with a few divine thoughts than to brood and imagine what might happen to me.

I have been in jails to visit people but never there in need of a visitor. I needed mercy; not that I had broken any law that I knew but merely because I was . . . in need of mercy, not even knowing why! Falsely accused! Me? Enter a country illegally? Never! Well almost never – but Sudan is a different story....

I had come to Ivory Coast to visit Christian literature outlets and acquaint them with the products we produced at Evangel Publishing House in Kenya.

The walls in my cell were a light yellow with no windows and only the door which had been locked behind me. There was a noise of a key in the door. That's when Mercy walked in. I don't know that was her name, but she came in with a pail and a mop. The door clunked and was locked behind her. She saw me reading my Bible and in English asked if I was a Christian. I explained that I was and what I was doing and whom I wanted to meet. She headed back for the door, knocked and said, "Wait here"—as though I had a choice.

She came back shortly, and said everything would be alright. My little Ghanian angel of mercy went on washing the floor, then left.

An hour later, I was out of jail, with the people I came to see, and was once again in the world of freedom. I thought of Joseph in prison and felt a parallel when I later reread the story in Genesis 39:21.

Mercy is when you find favour in the sight of God (Isaiah 19:19 and Genesis 60:10).

To find favour and mercy look to God. He has much to give and in various ways. The mercy I received was an English-speaking Ghanaian in a French speaking country. Works for me!

78

Selfish "Sacrifice"

You probably have had a similar experience. It's an experience many brides have as a result of wedding showers. Two toasters! Two coffee pots! There are several things which can be done of course. One can be kept as a backup. Or, it can be taken back for a refund. On the other hand, it can be stashed to be re-gifted, hopefully unrecognized, to the bride of the next wedding on the horizon.

I have lived long enough in our "more-than-we-need-society" to see the same gift circulate several times, until the packaging becomes a bit tacky—not to mention the warranty and style running out before it even gets used.

Many people give God the leftovers. When sacrifices were given to God in the Old Testament, it had to be the best of the flock, without spot or wrinkle. It was not the lamb with the broken leg or the bull with a blind eye.

Personally, I find it difficult to buy wedding gifts. Not because of the expense, but because of *what* to get. So, I leave it to my wife. She knows how to fit a gift to the person for whom it is intended. We don't hand on something which cost us little or nothing.

Did you hear about the thief who gave a tithe of all he stole to the church? Some sacrifice!

Yet we often give to God the least and the last: just leftovers.

Gad, a friend of King David, told him to go to make a sacrifice at a specific place to stop the plague that had come on Israel. When David got there the owner offered King David the whole deal. FREE! Threshing floor, oxen, wood from the yokes for the fire: he was offered everything for nothing. The king could have made a sacrifice which would have been no sacrifice at all. But we read in 2 Samuel 24:24-25 that David would not offer to the Lord something which cost him nothing.

How often have we handed over to God something that was worthless to us or that cost us little or nothing? When was the last time, before considering our own needs first, we gave the best to God?

Cal with mother

79

Rash Behaviour

I don't think I'm the only one who tried to speed up God's timetable. I know people who say they have been called of God to be a preacher. And it seems clear they do have a strong desire in their heart to minister to people. They are so urgent about it that they feel they have to get into a pulpit as a pastor before taking any appropriate training

With God's timing and a bit of patience that call could be fulfilled. Being sensitive to God is not always easy. To know what isn't quite enough. To know when is crucial!

How often do you see people actually plan ahead, think things through and make clear decisions in life before they take an important step? Most folk unfortunately take action based on a whim, an advertisement, an emotion or as a reaction to some inner personal turmoil, or because they "heard" that it was a good move to make.

Decisions can too often be made without consideration of the final repercussions, either in a person's own life or in the lives of many around them. Some of the most devastating results come from rash decisions.

Most of humanity has two methods of behaviour. Selfish or selfless! People often waffle between one or another direction. Others live consistently in one mode or the other. It's a rare person who is consistently selfless. Mother Teresa probably was one of those.

Human nature has never changed from Adam until right now. Adam and Eve both had a selfish streak when they wanted to "be like gods," as they were tempted by Satan. This pattern has not varied much since time began. God had uninhibited fellowship with Adam and Eve until they made a rash and selfish decision. That set up the whole human race for the fallen future.

Even the best of men and women have their moments of rash behaviour. God's chosen, King Saul, made a hasty and rash decision in 1 Samuel 13 which affected the whole tribe of Israel. He tried to get ahead of God.

And people do it collectively for selfish reasons. Just look at Acts 5:8, where it seems the only thoughtful one among the Sanhedrin was a man called Gamaliel. Rash decisions, even in a democratic atmosphere, can lead to very ugly results. Rash behaviour can be very embarrassing.

80 Leeches

When I was a child we holidayed in Muskoka, in northern Ontario where my father was raised as a child. It was while trying to catch little frogs for bait and wading in knee-deep murky watered that I discovered my first leeches. Dark, slimy, repulsive! With teensy weensy teeth and saliva which anaesthetises. They attach themselves to you and start sucking blood until they are gorged. You don't feel a thing—until you see them; then you scream with fear and horror (at least I did).

I was somewhat surprised later in life to read that historically leeches were used as a medical procedure. That seemed to pass into history as a medieval and superstitious practice. Until recently! The practice is now being revived, especially when medically reattaching severed fingers or ears which were accidentally detached. Some doctors have begun to attach leeches to remove engorged blood until new veins can grow to carry the flow of blood again.

Strange how modern science isn't always modern!

There are others kinds of leeches.

Human!

Victims are chosen quite carefully and deliberately. They select people with money or influence. They anaesthetise them with friendliness, flattery, compliments and little favours. Then they begin the sucking process. It often takes time before the victims realize they are being conned.

In Proverbs 30:15-16 we read, "*The leech has two daughters—Give and Give! There are three things that are never satisfied, Four never say, 'Enough!' The grave, The barren womb, The earth that is not satisfied with water—And the fire never says, 'Enough!'*"

Giving is a good thing when it is with discretion and wisdom. It's quite another thing to be leeched.

I didn't like it when I gave blood unwillingly to a leech. I don't like it when someone tells me a fraudulent story and bilks me for money which could have been used for a better cause.

Enough already!

81 Things

I saw her in Sudan. I saw similar people many times in Sudan. Yet this time it reached me at a depth to which it had never before penetrated. I stood there well-fed, well-clothed and owning a home in Canada. I have a car. My house is furnished. I have a spouse, children and grandchildren.

She stood in what I found out later was her only piece of clothing—a somewhat tattered, yet clean, light and flowered dress. She stood in an overgrown circle of what was left of part of a mud wall. It used to be her home. Her husband had been killed in a raid by the Arab Islamists from the north. Her children had been taken north as slaves.

What else did she have? A little bundle tied in an off-white piece of cloth which held who-knows-what, possibly a little food, and a staff for walking. That was the extent of her possessions. She had just returned from a refugee camp outside Sudan intending to try to pick up part of her life and go on living...somehow. Surprisingly, she had a smile on her face for a moment, which soon faded as she looked at the emptiness. She was a Christian. But she was grateful even for the empty land from which she had long before been driven.

When I returned to Canada I thought of her. She had life and not much more. I also thought of Canada and of us as Canadians and all the wonderful things we own. We have life too, but our view of what life is all about is dramatically different from that seeming helpless and hopeless woman in Sudan. Jesus said, *"for one's life does not consist in the abundance of the things he possesses"* (Luke 12:15).

All grown in our own backyard

Yet we in the western world seem forever to be acquiring more things, many of them of little or no real use and certainly of no eternal value. Why is it we always want more? We see something advertised on television and are often inclined to actually consider buying it. We WANT more things. We are even told "You deserve it!"

The prayer of the Psalmist was *"incline my heart to Your testimonies, And not to covetousness"* (Psalm 119:36).

Do we need a wake-up call? Is that what the recession of 2009 was all about?

82 Silence Can Be Wise

Stephen Mbiti worked for us as a house servant many years ago in Kenya. It was a colossal cost—$14 monthly. Mary's and my salaries combined amounted to $180 monthly.

But Stephen Mbiti was more than an employee. He had eyes like a hawk, and it was almost always his eyes which caught the movement of wild animals when I went hunting for our protein supply twice a year.

Even the best eyes fail from time to time. We were following a small herd of zebra into a bushy area hoping to find some wildebeest, which often herd together. On foot we stalked the zebra downwind, treading softly. Since I had the rifle, I led the way. Gestures and touches from Stephen guided me. Seeing the zebra was easy because of their colouring.

It was with shock and a shiver of fear that we suddenly realized we had walked into the middle of a herd of Cape buffalo. They are more aggressively dangerous than lions. We froze in the tropical heat. They had not yet caught our scent. Silence was absolutely essential. We had heard stories about this kind of situation. They did not have happy endings. We walked backwards one quiet and careful step at a time—very silently.

There are times when silence is great wisdom. Often love makes the difference. Proverbs 17:9 describes it well. *"He that covers a transgression seeks love, But he who repeats a matter separates very friends."*

People who awaken in the morning and set their mouths on "cruise" until bedtime are rarely, if ever, the most wise. Ecclesiastes 3:7 says everything has its time: *"A time to tear, And a time to sew; A time to keep silence, And a time to speak."* Many people would avoid confrontations if they'd just clam up.

Occasionally a person is told very rudely to "just shut up!"

Sometimes that's just plain good advice, though there are more kindly ways of saying it. Job put it this way: *"Oh, that you would be silent, and it would be your wisdom!"* (Job 13:5).

Have you ever heard the term "Silence is golden"?

83

The Good Life!

Going into life with goals, ambition and great expectations is normal. It should be.

What can be said against wanting to have a good income and a financially comfortable life? It's not wrong to be rich. I wouldn't mind it myself. Poverty is not as spiritual as some claim. Being in need and living by faith need not necessarily be a lifelong demand. Asceticism is of little real value either in the short or the long term. Rich is good and poverty is not good.

Yet there is more involuntary poverty than there ever will be intentional and honest riches. Honest riches seem in modern times to be less common than in previous generations. Something to do with our modern work ethic!

Those who are rich seem to pick up a lot of respect on the way to riches, not necessarily for their way of getting rich as much as for the riches themselves. Poverty has few real friends. People with a little more gall than the normal population go out of their way to cosy up to the rich. That's a pity. After a while the rich don't know who are really trying to be true friends and who are courting their dollars. Honour for the person is less than honour of the wealth.

And, speaking of honour, don't we all want to be respected, at least to some degree? No one enjoys rejection, disregard and downright rudeness! There is a vast difference between honour and reverence. Some folk try strenuously to create a reverent following. Such a waste of effort!

As some might say, "Get a life!" A person can be so wrapped up in pursuing riches, honour and their own version of the good life that they actually miss the best that life has to offer. Life becomes opaque when seen through a lens that is smeared with the marks of greasy grasping fingers.

Strange how the young want to be rich, the middle aged want a measure of honour, and the elderly start thinking more seriously about the fragility of life. The strange thing is, you can have it all if you have the right attitude. It's a matter of proportion.

But don't take my word for it. Just read Proverbs 22:4: *"By humility and the fear of the LORD Are riches and honour and life."*

84 Leadership Abilities

Being in leadership is not always as sweet and comfortable an experience as many imagine. Often tough decisions and genuine risk is needed for leaders. My experience as a junior missionary many years ago in Kenya made me realize this as I observed the difficult choices which often had to be made by individuals or committees. It led to my writing this little poem on July 10, 1976.

Cal & Mary's first missionary picture

"Sound the retreat,
I think we've been beat,"
Said the leader from somewhere behind.
For up at the fore
Midst the blood and the gore
This leader you seldom will find.

Yes, leaders are various
And some are nefarious
They're always so full of advice.
But to get in the fray
And to work and to pray
For themselves, it's not very nice.

It's always some other
Deeply committed poor brother
Who's advised to give all that he's got,
Not the one with the theory
Who's afraid to get weary,
Who'll risk getting put on the spot!

If you'd be a leader
And not just a reader
(Whoever you are, please take heed)
Then stop theorizing
And start realizing
You've Got To Get Out There and Lead!!

True leadership required the hands of the leaders to have some dirt under their fingernails at times. There's no such thing as a leader to whom every decision is clear, easy and automatic. If you have a lust for leadership, examine yourself closely since you might be working your way up to failure.

85 Is It Just "Luck"?

I have been told all my life that all men are equal. And yet once in a while, I find myself in a situation where I am tempted to believe otherwise.

All too often I have found myself in the middle of devastation and horror following a war, a flood, a hurricane or a famine. I have seen the blank expressions of despair in the eyes especially of parents unable to feed a starving child who is dying in their arms. I have seen those with arms and/or legs torn away by a land-mine or a scatter bomb. I have seen the remains of whole towns swept away by raging rivers or mudslides. My eyes have seen too much of it!

As a well-dressed Canadian, I know what it is to feel totally out of place among people in rags crowded into seething masses of displaced refugees. I live in a fine house in Canada, and they are crowded into makeshift shelters of grass, reeds and perhaps some sheared tin from some long gone house. I know what it feels like to return to my place for the night and have a proper meal. They are poor, and by comparison, I am very rich. Yet look at the equality reflected in Exodus 30:15.

The rich man is not worth one cent more nor the poor man less in the eyes of God—all men are equal. It's a level playing field. And from this firm basis of truth we must relate to the poor. It must be from a heart of the Christian "attitude of gratitude" to God for His abundant blessing on us that we should willingly obey. *"Defend the poor and fatherless; Do justice to the afflicted and needy"* (Psalm 82:3).

We have created class consciousness through our inability to accept the fact of our equal mortality with the poor. We find it difficult to obey what Jesus said in Luke 14:1. It was some years ago in Moscow that a Christian pastor told me that they pray for us in the West. "You are so preoccupied with *things*."

Can Jesus really be serious when He gives such an instruction? Yes! In fact, the word of God goes a little further, and neutralizes even our good works unless they are done in genuine love (1 Corinthians 13:3).

We somehow imagine we have created an almost perfect society in the West and we are closer to perfection than any other area of the world. Look at what Jesus said to one rich man in Matthew 19:21.

Things! What do they really mean? Our own attitude will determine that.

86

But I Thought...

Your physical ancestry is the same as every other human on the face of the earth. Monkeys, apes, primordial mud and genetic soup have nothing to do with it. I've often paralleled the behaviour of chickens with humans, but there is clearly no convergence.

We were all created by God, and God repeats the miracle with the birth of every child born on the face of the globe. Life is not like spontaneous combustion. You may have thought otherwise, but science has, with the study of mitochondria and DNA, proven that you and I are related. If that makes you feel bad, I'm sorry... and if I knew you personally I might not be too pleased myself. But we are related. It's a long story—about 6,000 years long.

Cal's mother - 1951

The issue of your physical ancestry is clear.

Let's have a look at your spiritual ancestry.

You were born into a specific family. That family has a specific history of good, bad and intriguing. There is the making of a book in every human family unit: functional, dysfunctional, good, bad and indifferent. Moms and dads have tremendous influence on their children, as do grandparents and other relatives. Certain traits and tendencies run in families—not just the jobs they do but also the way they think, act and interact with others.

What most people don't quite recognise is that there is a spiritual legacy in families, not just an inheritance through a last will and testament. That can be good or terrible. Reference is made to this in 2 Timothy 1:5.

Three generations - I'm the kid

Thank God for Eve! None of us would be here without her. Within the human family as a whole there are good and bad family units. If you come from a solid and well-balanced Christian family, you should probably get down on your knees and thank God.

Cal & brother David

Some might say, "But my parents and grandparents were Christian, I thought that tradition served me well, and besides, I go to church, too." Not the right thought. Did you ever question what a real Christian is? Why are some so much more peaceful and content than others?

The answer is simple. It's because they have a *relationship* with God through knowing the resurrected Jesus. Do you?

If not, you should get down on your knees and ask God to take you into His family through Jesus Christ. It may be the beginning of a brand new sane and solid hierarchy of faith. Let's call it your spiritual DNA!

87 Did You Ever Wonder?

People have vowed to kill me. It's simply because I told the truth about what has and is happening in Sudan at the hands of Islamist fanatics. I'm not the first!

There are a few things in Scripture for which I really wish I had an answer. I'm not wondering about a doctrinal issue in this instance. It's about the rash words of a few rogues who had it in for the apostle Paul. You may have read the story in the book of Acts.

Paul had gone to Jerusalem, went about his normal activities of teaching and preaching, having fellowship with the saints there, and at the same time observing all the rules of the synagogue. Some of the leaders of the Jews made it tough on Paul, so much so that he was in jail over a very nebulous religious accusation. Paul was one from that new-fangled religion who had "turned the world upside-down" according to his accusers.

Forty men bound themselves by an oath to kill Paul. These were religious people. These were people who read one of the Ten Commandments—"You shall not murder." Yet they vowed that they would not eat or drink until they had killed Paul. For their sake I hope they had a heavy meal before the set out to fulfil their oath!

The scheme was heard of by Paul's nephew and conveyed to Paul who sent his nephew to the Roman ruler, who in turn called out a mass of soldiers to escort Paul away from Jerusalem in the dark of night. Ha!

Did you ever wonder what happened to those forty men? Two years later, plans were still in the making to kill Paul. But in the meantime, what did these potential murderers have to eat? Their own words!

James 5:12 warns against such foolish commitments.

It's tough to have to eat your own words. There's no sustenance in rash words and promises. To swear an oath is a very serious step to take. It may not seem of any great significance in these days, but an oath is an oath, then and now. I wonder what they discussed in their next planning meeting. I wonder which of the forty began to sneak a bit of food first!

And oath or a vow at a wedding is just as important, even in Hollywood. But how many eat their words after they've eaten the wedding cake?

The ungodly live by the world's standard. They'll make up their own rules resulting in emptiness in their souls until they do find solace, forgiveness and life through Jesus Christ.

I'm still alive. God has His ways.

88

Sneaky Snake

Some years ago, I was on Ruzinga Island on a preaching mission, and it was my joy to see many come to a personal knowledge of Jesus Christ as Saviour. One of those was the father of my very good friend with whom I had travelled, Odhiambo Okite. One afternoon, Odhiambo and I decided to go swimming on the shores of his home island in Lake Victoria.

To my surprise the sand on the shore was black from volcanic stone gradually worn by waves and weather. It was calm and beautiful. There were occasional rocks spotted about on the narrow strip of sandy shore. I was sitting on one with my back to Lake Victoria as I began to take off my shoes. Odhiambo was sitting on a rock which nestled up close to some overhanging foliage and the trunk of a tree. His shoes were off and we were in conversation. I glanced up and my blood froze. A cobra was poised within inches of the back of Odhiambo's neck. He saw the look in my eyes as I said, "Don't move!"

He froze. His eyes were wide and questioning, somehow aware that he was in grave danger but not knowing what it was. The cobra had begun to sway back and forth behind Odhiambo's neck. I quietly instructed him to very slowly lean forward, pick up his shoes and creep away from the danger. "VERY slowly," I repeated. He did as instructed and when he looked back the snake was slithering off into the foliage.

Had that snake struck Odhiambo in the back of the neck he would have been dead in less than a minute. We didn't go swimming. We started talking about snakes, including the worst one. And he's out to deceive us all, as he did Adam and Eve. It's worth looking at 2 Corinthians 11:3. The problem with that snake is that he's sneaky and often uses an indirect approach, taking advantage of vulnerable or gullible people and circumstances (Psalm 140:1-3). He also deceives and kills in other ways (Proverbs 23:31-32). There is also the babbling gossip Satan uses (Ecclesiastes 10:11). Yet his end is assured (Revelation 12:9).

Meanwhile, we have this assurance in Luke 10:19: *"Behold, I give you the authority to trample on serpents and scorpions, and over all the power of the enemy, and nothing shall by any means hurt you."* Also look at Psalm 91:13.

We simply need to keep our eyes peeled to see the danger before it strikes. We need to look out for each other.

We simply need to keep our eyes peeled to see the danger before it strikes. We need to look out for each other.

89 Uncertain Riches

I have neither been underpaid nor overpaid. I have never asked for a rise in pay.

I have often thought what I might do if I had more income, but it has rarely been a pro-longed thought. In reflecting on this after these many years, I have, like Paul, both been in want and at other times abounded. In neither case has it been a hardship. When you learn to live inside the bounds of your income, it's not hard to do without your wants.

Proverbs 23:4 says: *"Do not overwork to be rich; Because of your own understanding, cease!"* I have been accused, and will admit to a degree that I am a little bit of a workaholic, somewhat—maybe. But it has never been for my own gain. Inactivity does not fit me very well. It causes me to gain weight and lose initiative. I work at things which are worthwhile in the long term—like—say, eternity. It's not a conscious, "treasures in heaven" motive.

I have come to the conviction that I was not placed on this earth to be the centre of the universe but to serve God and others even in what seems mundane at times. Why? I really don't care what my grave clothes will cost. That will be out of my hands in any case. What does strike me as brilliant and meaningful is found in Proverbs 23:5: *"Will you set your eyes on that which is not? For riches certainly make themselves wings; They fly away like an eagle toward heaven."*

Near the end of 2008 we saw that clearly illustrated.

So why waste so much effort in selfish gain when we can in fact, with the right attitude and motives, inflict the world with GOOD? Yes, and gain eternal rewards for being selfless and serving.

Why should people like Mother Teresa be so few in the world?

Is it perhaps that too many people cannot get their eyes off this world and realize the heavenly?

90 Advice

A young lady who was just graduating from grade eight asked me, along with many others, to write a word of advice for her classmates going into high school. I reflected on it for some time then came up with the following, which was published in *The Way They Should Go* by Kirsten Femson:

"Wisdom is the principal thing; Therefore get wisdom. And in all your getting, get understanding" (Proverbs 4:7).

We live in an age when wisdom is lacking. Yet it is the principal thing. It should be our greatest quest. It must be at the top of our "wish list" yet it cannot be had by wishing. It can only be had by a diligent seeking after God. Above everything else, including riches and fame, Solomon asked God for wisdom. We read in Ecclesiastes 7:25 the value of practical wisdom: *"I applied my heart to know, To search and seek out wisdom and the reason of things, To know the wickedness of folly, even of foolishness and madness."*

Never be afraid to ask questions. Everything about our life, our world and our universe is created by God, and understood through the wisdom that God alone can give. Sometimes we understand things by faith, and that too is great wisdom.

What you must understand is that for any true comprehension of the world around us, we must be in a right relationship with God. Theories, ideas and propositions which sound good, may come from even the greatest intellects but until they are purified through the cauldron of God's Word and the wisdom of His Word, none of it will stand the test of time. In Proverbs 11:30 we read,

"The fruit of the righteous is a tree of life, And he who wins souls is wise."

Life will throw some severe curves at you, but every one of them can be handled if we trust the source and use the wisdom God freely gives us. *"If any of you lacks wisdom, let him ask of God, who gives to all liberally and without reproach, and it will be given to him"* (James 1:5).

Never be afraid to ask!

91

It Can't Happen To Us!

I thought it would never happen to me. I had heard of "careless" people suffering severe cuts from chainsaws. I was very careful. Not me! Well, not until my chainsaw would not decelerate, touched a tree then bounced to a rock and then toward my left leg. Fifteen stitches!

In meetings I sometimes speak about the disastrous civil war, manipulated famine and genocide taking place against the black Sudanese population by the extremist Jihadist Muslims of the Khartoum regime. I had seen how terrorism was an everyday reality. Death was all around.

People come up to me afterward saying such things as, "I never realized how bad it was." or "I'm certainly glad we don't experience terror like that!" Then of course 9/11 hit, and the hearts and emotions of every person in North America were scrambled and terrified. Suddenly what seemed to be an impossibility was a stark and horrifying

reality. A relative of mine lived through that horror, but lost hundreds of colleagues. He knew them personally, either on a face to face basis or in a telephone relationship.

Horror and disaster *can* come home. Yet many people live an uninformed and insular life, and what happens in other parts of the world is merely an item on the evening news. When Job had three "comforters" trying to show him that he had some hidden sin or unrighteousness, he pointed out their own misinformed attitude as judgmental.

In Job 12:5, Job answers his critics by saying *"A lamp is despised in the thought of one who is at ease; It is made ready for those whose feet slip."* (The word "lamp" in this verse is often translated from the Hebrew "disaster," which fits what Job is trying to relate).

While many people are at ease in North America they fail to realize that they are standing on slippery ground. I have often been told that I shouldn't take the chances I do in going to the troubled nation of Sudan. The ground is no more slippery there than here. But terror has come home to North America now! Jesus said, in Matthew 5:45: *"for He [God] makes His sun rise on the evil and on the good, and sends rain on the just and on the unjust."* No one is scot-free when it comes to trouble—no matter how righteous they might be. And we have God's own testimony to the fact that Job was righteous above all men in his time.

No one is scot-free when it comes to trouble... the rain still falls on the just and the unjust.

Yes, God puts a hedge of protection around His children but the rain still falls on the just and the unjust. I am not trying to scare anyone, but Jesus did say, *"These things I have spoken to you, that in Me you may have peace. In the world you will have tribulation; but be of good cheer, I have overcome the world"* (John 16:33).

92 Church Malady

My grandson has a speaking disorder. Note: "disorder" is the key word here. Rather than use proper English grammar as taught in the local Baptist academy which he attends, he uses the language of the larger population in town. "Like, you know Luke! Well, him and me went to the skateboard park." *"Him and me"?* Give me a break! He has been cajoled, corrected and taught the right way of saying, "He and I went...." We have suggested, commanded and ORDERED him to speak English properly.

He either doesn't care or is deliberately disobedient. He is sixteen—the usual age to be a little rebellious, self-directed and careless about the finer things of life. Everyone is on his case, yet he persists in this malady. It's a teenage disorder. All his peers are much the same. He would do well to read the book *English as She Are Spoke.* My daughter jokingly told him that unless he learned both English and French properly, the only job that could be open to him would be prime minister of Canada. He's starting to correct himself now before we correct him. There's hope!

But is the Church of Jesus Christ any better? I think not. *Having itching ears we heap to ourselves over-the-edge teachers.* They speak about faith in extra-biblical ways, reducing God's answers to prayers based on a formula. They teach "specialties" in doctrine with emphasis on the sensational, the carnal little sound bites and the glitz that appeals to human nature rather than spiritual challenge and growth. Shallow.

The Bible instructs us to preach the whole council of God, not the sensationalism which appeals only to the senses. This is not to say that God does nothing sensational. He does. But all God does is based on the solid foundation of His Word, His character and His will. But when something is sensational, we capitalize on it. It has become a malady in the Church.

Would to God we had more people with a clear cut convictions as Balaam, God's prophet who said, *"I could not go beyond the word of the LORD my God, to do less or more"* (Numbers 22:18).

There are some areas in church life where there have been so many add-ons or subtractions that the Church is only faintly visible. My father once made the statement, "What God does needs no exaggeration." He probably wrote that as reminder to himself, but it's good advice for us all.

The Church has only one foundation and one Head. The Church needs to be Head-strong!

93 Servants of God

My wife, Mary, and I went into a Hindu temple many years ago in Kisumu, Kenya. We basically went out of curiosity but also to observe the manner of the Hindus in their form of religion and worship. It was very educational and very interesting to see the various gods with their semi-human, semi-animal appearances. For a Christian, it was also somewhat disconcerting. We couldn't relate to these strange idols. We observed little sweet cakes and bits of food sitting in front of some of the idols.

The priest who was showing us around invited us to eat some of the offerings made to these idols. My wife is somewhat of an experimenter with foods of many cultures, and she serves various international dishes at home. Without thinking, Mary reached to take a small bit to taste. I whispered a few words into her ear and she didn't pick up the food. We continued our tour and left shortly afterward better informed and somewhat subdued. It came to mind that it was not so much the act of eating food offered to idols but the possible repercussion in the life of a weaker Christian who may have observed (1 Corinthians 8:8 and Acts 15:28-29).

News conference in Ottawa

Being a servant of God can have what might be perceived as disadvantages. We are observed and often seen as role models. Sometimes we fail. I know with certainty that I have failed often. Others have been observed in the headlines around the world, and the seeds of doubt and confusion are planted in the souls of many, particularly weaker Christians who are not grounded solidly in God's Word.

First Kings 13 is a story of a servant of God who, deceived by another servant of God (see verse 13), was led into direct disobedience to God's specific instructions. The results were catastrophic.

We don't need to live under a legalistic obsession with every action being examined for rectitude. But we do need to be sure that our actions are observably obedient to God's word and will. A servant of God called to ministry and public scrutiny is often under the magnifying glass.

The overriding law of God is love. It covers a multitude of sins, yes! But it always puts interest and concern for others first.

It's a tough row to hoe, but it's the only way to assure fruit in your ministry.

College 50th anniversary - Witnesses Class

94 It's the Nature of the Beast!

Being a preacher's kid is not the easiest role in life. I was one and I have two.

My father, a well-respected pastor and church official, was easy to live with. His spankings were few but very certain and never without cause. His reprimands were with conviction and force. Yet his leadership in the home was filled with love, humour, fun and genuine good times. There was plenty of attention and very little tension.

But being a preacher's kid exposes you to all kinds of scrutiny, judgment and rather high and holy expectations from the church members. As a teenager I recall a telephone call to my parents reporting on me from one of the congregants. I had been seen walking down the main street *holding hands* with a blonde girl wearing *lipstick!* I guess I was on my way to hell. Dad's comment was "Was she pretty?"

People normally complimented my parents on their five children. Their response was, "Wait until they have grown up and married." They waited, and we're all serving God.

Genetics aside, parents have a great deal to do with where their offspring land when they leave their influence. The direction they take is about 97 percent environmentally influenced. That means "home and social environment." The other three percent is buried somewhere in the DNA.

Yet even under the best of circumstances, kids, including preacher's kids, do have a mind of their own and often take a leap in the wrong direction and associate with questionable others. It's the nature of the beast. Look at Eli's two sons in 1 Samuel 2:12 -17. They may have agreed with the song "I did it my way."

There are casualties. But this is most often brought about by bad parental example or sheer rebellion. Good and successful parenting is possible even by instinct, without all the books on parenting. There doesn't have to be so many casualties. Children can be nurtured. The "beast" can be trained.

I once saw a man in Addis Ababa near the emperor's home in Ethiopia leading three African lions down the sidewalk on leashes. Constraints on children will not kill them.

Leashes are not bad. Paul said something similar in 1 Timothy 3:1-3.

95 My Courtship

My wife of over 53 years, Mary, didn't play "hard to get," but it was an uphill struggle trying to win her heart, especially since at the time she thought her heart belonged to someone else. She discovered all by herself that was not so. That's when I turned on the afterburners in our courtship. My ardour was unlimited except by my wallet. And others were in that race too.

Mary, October 1970

We met at college. I brought Mary to my home for the traditional family inspection, and I was subjected to the same scrutiny in her home. When the time came for our relationship to go to another level, I was just old-fashioned enough to ask her father if I could have his daughter's hand in mar-

College graduation, 1959, EPBC

riage. I'll never forget that scene. He looked at me, measuring me up with a feigned and somewhat critical eye, and after a long pause, he said, "Well, I guess you're the best of the crummy lot." The answer was a strange sort of "yes." Then, knowing I was going into Christian ministry, he added, "You might just as well not support her as I." I came to love his sense of humour.

High school, Oshawa

I could have danced all night—except that I didn't know how to dance.

We have an enduring relationship.

Our relationship with God should be just as enthusiastic and filled with adoration. Deuteronomy 4:29 comes to mind. It can be an "all your heart" matter or just a passing fancy.

Your relationship with God will make your heart dance even when your feet can't keep up.

Cal, 1955, Fairbanks

96 Rules and Spanking

I've given this a lot of thought. This may not be "politically correct," but I am generally getting sick and tired of people having to shade and manipulate the truth in order to be politically correct. In some places, you can go to jail for simply telling the truth plainly. But I'm going to tell the truth here. I spanked my children. We had rules in our home. We love our children; that's why the rules and the spanking.

I didn't beat them or abuse them. I spanked them for disciplinary reasons. When they were of a "reasoning age" both Mary and I reasoned with them. You can ask either my son John or my daughter Elaine whether they were abused and I'm quite sure they'll probably tell you that looking back now they would thank me. In fact my son has already thanked me for the times of discipline.

Both of them serve God and live and think right. They are a danger to no one but the devil. We have an excellent relationship filled with love and open communication. Our family is very close-knit. We often have differing opinions now that my son is a man and my daughter a woman.

But I spanked them! Perhaps some of our "politically correct" politicians and social workers need a good spanking. Not abuse: just a good spanking. It would be good for them.

God has rules with his family too, simply because He loves us. The rules He sets in place according to Deuteronomy 6:24 are *"for our good always"* (emphasis added). We are told that whom God loves He chastens.

Look at Hebrews 12:7-11.

It seems fairly obvious to me that our rebellious society today may well be due to a lack of loving chastening.

Kids and goats, 1977

97 Fearing God

When I was a child I think I just may have had a better understanding of the fear of the Lord. When I did something wrong and my mother discovered it, I might hear the words "You wait until your father comes home!" Father always came home. And in fear and trembling I would await the judgment. He was very fair in his punishments, and they were seldom more than I knew I deserved. Sometimes I blamed my brother...that only rarely worked – for a while.

Job's comforting critics had seven days while they wept and comforted Job in total silence. But somewhere in those seven days they became less comforting and more critical in their judgments. And in turn they all told him what the problem was. They took it upon themselves to rationalize why Job found himself in this terrible condition.

Job listened to their long analysis with "the patience of Job." And he had a much more sound answer than their accusations. You should read the pertinent questions Job asked his critics in Job 13:7-11. Read them slowly and thoughtfully. It ends with: "*Will not His excellence make you afraid, And the dread of Him fall upon you?*"

How often we all find ourselves assessing the unfortunate saying, "They brought it on themselves!" In some cases that may very well appear to be true. But I have yet to meet a person who knows every possible thought and action and the good and bad of another person. Most of us don't even understand ourselves fully, let alone others. Yet we judge as though we were God.

Will it be well when He searches ***you*** out? A true fear of God, even a dread or terror of the Lord, is not unbecoming. Since the Second Coming of Jesus Christ could very well be soon, we need to get out of that mindset. Isaiah prophecies about the Day of the Lord when in Isaiah 2:10 he advises: *"Enter into the rock, and hide in the dust, From the terror of the LORD And the glory of His majesty."*

"He that is without sin first cast a stone" (John 8:7 KJV).

When we stop long enough to think about it, we all deserve a few lumps on our heads and we'd more often have them if God in mercy did not intervene. Just another thought, if you don't mind: it might be a good idea for all of us to shut our traps before we are caught in our own traps.

There is such a thing as a healthy fear of God. That's just another part of wisdom.

98 Law and Politics

Political decisions bring about changes in law. Sometimes total confusion follows.

A friend of mine, Samuel Odunaike, an executive with Shell Oil in Nigeria, told me of the day in Lagos when a change in law required everyone to switch from driving on the left side of their road to the right side. A specific day was chosen. It was total confusion. It ended with a gridlock where thousands of people simply locked their cars where they were jammed in the streets and walked home. It took weeks to get it all straightened out. They might as well have been in a wilderness.

Unfortunately many politicians are less dependable than the weather. National laws grow out of the political arena. The structure and content of law has become so infiltrated with the currying of favour to special interest groups that it has become an almost impossible task to interpret it within the context of its original intent.

I have heard Christians express concern that recent laws are becoming more and more restrictive to the biblical view, and freedom of speech and religion are slowly being eroded. I have to agree.

There is no doubt that there are politicians who help form laws which they genuinely believe are good for the general public. Then someone challenges the meaning and spirit of that new law, and a new law or amendment is necessary, which further complicates its interpretation. There is little doubt that some politicians clearly oppose wise biblical morality, ethics and Christian standards.

The results are laws that are contradictory, vague, hard to impose or difficult to live with. Laws have become a great morass of shadows and mirrors.

Why? When people depart from the laws of God, they lose common sense. In Job 12:24, we read that God takes action when people forsake His laws; *"He takes away the understanding of the chiefs of the people of the earth, And makes them wander in a pathless wilderness."*

Mary, Elaine, Cashew, in Kenya

Don't take for granted that things will get better. Not unless you yourself are willing (and able) to step into the fray while still holding on to your biblical convictions and common sense with wisdom.

Wisdom comes from God. It very rarely comes from a majority vote.

99 Destiny

I often reflect on the course life takes. Reflections are good. Looking back to see the pattern life has taken reveals unexpected twists and turns. The strange voices and melodies of an unwritten symphony which produced what you are today and will continue into the unknown future are unpredictable. Look in the mirror of your soul today and see if you are satisfied with where and what you are. You are the reflection of everything you have allowed to influence your life.

Is it the best we can do to dance to the tunes which currently are hammered at us by our tilted society?

Who writes those tunes? This is perhaps one of the great questions which needs an answer. At some point, everyone needs to decide just who the fiddler is and whose tune they dance to. There are a myriad of possibilities.

Parents often direct the course of a child's life. Schoolmates introduce another raucous beat and rhythm. Education opens the ears to a whole galaxy of conflicting sounds and potentials. Associates add new airs and songs. The workplace often brings a new and too often boring and repetitive drumbeat. Some are merry, others mournful and some humdrum. So many voices!

Whose tune can do us the most good in the end?

Each influence brings new facets to light, new decisions to make and new challenges to face. The very fibre of life, good and bad, is affected by the various tunes, rhythms, strains and melodies which catch our attention, some of which we hold to most tenaciously. And each of those influences is a voice calling us to our eventual destiny.

Destiny is decided by decisions. Not just one, but many decisions. What we are today is a direct result of those decisions. What we will be down the road will be the result of decisions.

Perhaps a lingering glance at Deuteronomy 8:7-19 might give us a good lead on the tune, the voice, to which we should dance in life. Because, as in verse 16, it's *"to do you good in the end"* that really counts.

100 Trusting Others

Living in a fishbowl situation on a mission station in Africa has its advantages. Fellowship, advice and communal prayer are not the least of these. It also has some disadvantages. Sometimes you can get to know too much about other missionaries, and there creeps in a tendency to be judgmental, critical and even alienating because of perceived faults.

A rare fishing adventure on Lake Ontario

June 11, 2006

Variety is the spice of life. Some people represent a bland vanilla pudding, while others represent a chili pepper. They don't really mix too well. Yet both are a part of the human diet: just so with missionaries.

None of us ever agrees with everything another says and does, though some wisely avoid a confrontation on a minor matter. Even major differences can be discussed, and agreements can be made to disagree. But to castigate, marginalise and boycott another for their particular difference is neither necessary nor Christian.

As children of God, we have various gifts, callings and personalities. God has called us all to serve Him in one capacity or another. Reflecting on that incident, I have decided to learn to trust the Holy Spirit in others. I have no exclusive claim to rightness or righteousness. Numbers 12:9-10 are a good couple of verses to read in this regard.

Tuna caught of Mombasa

As Christians, we have to realize that the Holy Spirit who dwells in us is the same Holy Spirit who dwells in other Christians.

Could we possible be so arrogant that we feel the work and expression of God is more purely filtered through *our* lives and minds more than through the lives of any other Christian?

Spiritual pride destroys relationships.

101 Obey That Impulse!

As I stepped into the banquet room, I was awestruck. Gorgeous chandeliers, a large ornate table with matching antique chairs and paintings worth a mint! Such beauty I had rarely seen anywhere. This was the hall where the king of Spain had small intimate banquets with about thirty to forty people. I had never seen anything like this except in a museum. This place was in current use.

I had been invited to Spain to present the case for Christians to start using television to reach their own people for Christ Jesus. This famous restaurant was owned by a Christian, and the banquet was "on the house" for about twenty-five leading evangelical Spanish Christians. After a marvellous meal I made my presentation. Basically, I was urging them to get together and as a group of leaders, use television to present the gospel. It was then open for discussion.

I had a Spanish interpreter, a graduate of Oxford University, giving me a running translation of all that was said. I was left out of the discussion, and no questions were asked of me. The discussion became more animated, with a growing animosity among many of them. I was familiar with Latin temperament, but this seemed to be getting out of hand. Some of the things interpreted for me were almost unbelievable, almost hateful. And these were Christian leaders! I sat stunned for quite a while listening to the recriminations. Such repulsive and harsh words I had seldom heard.

Then I had my own impulse. I knew it was from God but I was somewhat frightened to obey. After some hesitation I turned to my interpreter, asking him to stand with me. I stood suddenly to my feet, which got their attention. I was thinking, "What right have I to interrupt the top Christian leaders of Spain?"

I began with an expression of horror at what I was hearing and then read from John 17, with particular emphasis on verse 21.

I spoke rather emphatically and plainly. After about ten minutes I sat down, wondering what I had got myself into. There was dead silence for about a minute or two. I was on tenterhooks, thinking I was likely to be rejected.

Suddenly one of the men dropped his head onto his arms on the table and began to sob, then another... and another. Men began to stand, walking around the table, crying on each other's shoulders and asking forgiveness. A peace and calm came into the room because the King had arrived by His Spirit. The meeting was a success.

When your impulse is from God, obey it. Avoid most other impulsive actions.

102 The Voice of God

Without giving it much thought I pointed my finger in his face and asked, "Why have you come in here to spy on what we are doing to help these other refugees?" His eyes suddenly bulged and he fled the church in an almost mad rush. The voice of the Spirit of God had subtly warned me in my own spirit that I was facing a dangerous man. But, as the Bible says, *"there are...so many kinds of voices in the world"* (1 Corinthians 14:10 KJV). But there is also the *right voice!*

"Son of Sam" in the United States killed people because he, purportedly, heard voices telling him to do so. Every father whose name was Sam in those days must have had a chill tingle down their spine when they thought with gratitude that it wasn't their son who became that serial killer. There are wrong voices!

There were a few other sons of 'Sam' who must have been listening to similarly perverse voices. It's recorded in the Bible in 1 Samuel. They suffered somewhat the same fate as the famous "Son of Sam" of more modern history. When Samuel was young and apprenticed to Eli, the priest who was father to those ancient "sons of Sam," he heard a voice, repeatedly. At first he didn't recognise it as God's voice. After all, there are many voices in the world.

As Christians we all go through that process of learning to recognise the voice of the Master. It often takes time to get used to the developing intimacy with God.

I never hear audible voices except when live people speak to me. Some of them I would rather not have heard! God speaks to me. The voice is within my spirit. It's neither weird nor unusual. And that "voice" within, when obeyed, always brings a blessing on someone—sometimes even on myself. More often it results in someone else receiving something from God, which might revolutionize their life or circumstances.

Jesus said in John 10:27, *"My sheep hear My voice, and I know them, and they follow Me."*

Do you?

103 Wisdom

I have problems with the use of the word "wisdom." People have told me I am wise. Others have gone overboard in their "praise" of my "wisdom." As a result, I've given it a lot of thought. The fact is that I have sometimes been a little envious of the wisdom exhibited by people much younger and less educated than myself.

My conclusion is that wisdom is not a *resident* and overriding quality in anyone. It comes and it goes with various occasions and circumstances. It is a quality to covet earnestly. We are urged to ask God for wisdom, and Solomon in the Proverbs urges us to seek it, covet it and strive for it.

I know that I have handled some situations with a modicum of wisdom. Yet at other times, by later personal assessment, I have acted foolishly...and not just when I was young.

It's true that in a practical sense knowledge and experience can and do lend themselves to wise decisions. But true wisdom is elusive even to those who are reputed to be wise.

The most consistently wise people I know are those who have an intimate relationship with God and His Word. The wisdom of this world is foolishness with God. Manipulated ideas backed with great oratorical skills may convince some people for a while, but when the haze and dust of those skills fall to the ground there remains simply—truth.

Truth, life and the way to wisdom is found only in Jesus Christ. No thought, advice or action can be considered wise until it is filtered through the Word of God, which is chiselled in stone—in the Rock of Ages (James 3:17, Proverbs 1:7).

Brains don't produce wisdom. God does.

This may be the wisest thing I ever wrote.

Bayridge Books Titles Include:

Counterfeit Code: Answering The Da Vinci Code Heresies (James Beverley)

More Faithful Than We Think (Lloyd Mackey)

Save My Children (Emily Wierenga)

Wars Are Never Enough: The Joao Matwawana Story (John Keith)

Award-winning Castle Quay Titles Include:

[illegible] Castle Quay [illegible] include:

Bent Hope (Tim Huff)

The Beautiful Disappointment (Colin McCartney)

The Cardboard Shack Beneath the Bridge (Tim Huff)

Certainty (Grant Richison) - NEW

The Chicago Healing Quest (Rose)

Dancing with Dynamite (Tim Huff) - NEW

Deciding to Know God in a Deeper Way (Sam [illegible]) - NEW

The Defilers (Deborah Gyapong)

Father to the Fatherless (Paul Boge)

[illegible] They Said (Arnold Bowler) - NEW

Jesus and Caesar (Brian Stiller)

Keep On Standing (Darlene Polachic)

The Leadership Edge (Elaine Stewart-Rhude)

Making Your Dreams Your Destiny (Judy Rushfeldt)

Mentoring Wisdom ([illegible]) - NEW

Mere Christian (Michael Coren)

One Smooth Stone (Marcia Lee Laycock)

Red Letter Revolution (Colin McCartney)

Seven Angels for Seven Days (Angelina Fast-Vlaar)

Stop Preaching and Start Communicating (Tony [illegible]) - NEW

Through Fire & Sea (Marilyn Meyers)

To [illegible] My Land (Elaine Rohin [illegible])

Vision that Works (David Collins)

Walking Towards Hope (Paul Boge)

What Happens When I Die (Brian Stiller) - NEW

The Way They Should Go (Kirsten Femson)

[illegible] Never Know What You Have Till You Give It Away (Brian Stiller) - NEW

www.ingramcontent.com/pod-product-compliance
Lightning Source LLC
Chambersburg PA
CBHW072045090426
42733CB00032B/2269
9781894860536